PEACE CORPS VICTIM

A Peace Corps Volunteer Story of Trauma and Betrayal

PATRICK SHEA RPCV

 FriesenPress

One Printers Way
Altona, MB R0G 0B0
Canada

www.friesenpress.com

Copyright © 2024 by Patrick Shea RPCV
First Edition — 2024

All rights reserved.

No part of this publication may be reproduced in any form, or by any means, electronic or mechanical, including photocopying, recording, or any information browsing, storage, or retrieval system, without permission in writing from FriesenPress.

ISBN
978-1-03-830814-6 (Hardcover)
978-1-03-830813-9 (Paperback)
978-1-03-830815-3 (eBook)

1. BIOGRAPHY & AUTOBIOGRAPHY, PERSONAL MEMOIRS

Distributed to the trade by The Ingram Book Company

Dedicated to Deborah Gardner.
There is no peace in the Peace Corps.

Name Changes

All names have been changed in order to protect the innocent from retaliation from the US Government and the Peace Corps. The location and time are in the Republic Georgia in the year 2016-2017. Nothing else has been changed.

Motivation

A portion of the proceeds will be going to helping Non-Governmental Organizations, the country of Georgia, to the developing world, and to select Georgian families. The author is doing this to protect future volunteers and bring about change by showing the reality of serving in the Peace Corps. Personal motivation of this work is for the author to find closure and to close this chapter of his life.

Publishing Disclaimer

The views expressed by the author are solely the views of the author and no other parties involved in the publishing or distribution of this book.

For Grammar Purists

Please understand this was written during COVID-19, while under martial law, through the outbreak of nearby wars, and while living in the developing world within the former Soviet Union in Georgia, and in isolation. I've spent a great deal on having the book published, if not professionally edited, with the knowledge that it is grammatically unshowered and unshaven.

Message from the Author

To anyone who doubts me: The Country Director of Peace Corps Georgia resigned his position the following year after I was discharged, well within the five-year limit, and was replaced with an Interim Director. From all reports I have heard, the departure was abrupt and messy to say the least. Country Directors are given the same options as the volunteers, to resign or be terminated. The Office of Inspector General of the Peace Corps has reports on this individual from multiple sources within the Peace Corps, if they have not destroyed them or tampered with them. On an unrelated note, anyone can look up a volunteer's Description of Service in the Library of Congress. All Peace Corps Description of Service documents are signed by a Country Director.

INTRODUCTION TO A PEACE CORPS COVER UP

Whistleblowers are not prosecuted by the US Government, they are persecuted. Writing this has cost me everything, but I cannot live in silence for what they did to me. To live in silence is to agree with them. I know they have and will treat others the same way. They did it to me, they have done it to others, and they left me no choice. I gave up everything to write this. I sold all my possessions and used up my life's savings for this. If anything comes from this, it will be used to help the developing world including, Georgia, Georgian families, and those at risk of victimization. I cannot live in silence knowing what they did to me. I have become the worst fate imaginable, a silent victim.

Writing this and it has taken a psychological and physical toll on me. The amount of time in energy put into this is staggering. There is nothing left to me after I almost died for the Peace Corps and America while serving, harassed by another volunteer to the point of assault, abused, intimidated, manipulated behind closed doors by the Peace Corps, threatened with criminal prosecution by the Peace Corps' Victim's Response into silence, denied medical care, and then forced to pay for my own injuries sustained while in the Peace Corps. The Peace Corps has taken years from my life, beyond what I served. I used to be such a proud volunteer; I was happy to serve my country.

I spent my life doing volunteer work since the seventh grade, not missing a Sunday of Church in twenty years, graduating top of my class with honors, even thanking every veteran I met, only to deal with this. Everything has stopped. My life has come to an end, and I cannot move forward anymore. I have been in torment dealing with these memories, trapped in a psychological hell blaming myself for everything. I am stuck reliving my past and I am isolated, living in fear, and I am not going to take it anymore. All of this has been burned into my memory.

My own community, many Returned Peace Corps Volunteers, refused to listen to me, they denied what happened to me. There were a few who told me to tell this story. When I speak, my own community dismisses me and tells me to be silent. I cannot function in America anymore. I have no trust for any of them. I had flashbacks, I blamed myself to the point I put a shotgun in my mouth. Why did I feel guilty, despite the fact I loved my country? The Peace Corps victim blamed me, they abused me with threats and manipulation tactics behind closed doors. They blamed me, and I was a victim. I went through hell for them, believing in them, and they did this to me. This is the Peace Corps.

The Peace Corps' main priority is their image and they bury reports to the point volunteers are afraid to report anything. The Peace Corps will continue to do everything they did to me, to others, they will continue to hide the truth, abuse victims, and victim blame. They will break their own laws and hide it behind closed door threats. Here is my Peace Corps experience. To anyone who is listening, I almost died for them, and I no longer care.

Patrick Shea – Returned Peace Corps Victim

ORIENTATION

DEAR VOLUNTEER

You will know the value of peace when you have a shotgun in your mouth. The Peace Corps threatened me after I almost died for them and they ruined my life. I used to believe America was the greatest country on Earth. I spent my life doing volunteer work, and doing the best I could to make the world a better place. If you are planning on serving, or are already in, ask yourself the hard questions. How far are you willing to go to help someone? Are you prepared to lose your life? Are you prepared to lose everything and go through the hell that I went through? There was a time in my life where I would have given my life for America, and I nearly did. I did not know the reality of what would happen to me. The Peace Corps is only an image. Here is my story.

Before I even stepped into the Republic of Georgia of Eastern Europe, my country of service in the US Peace Corps, I was already in love with it. I had the luck of having one of my childhood friends come from Tbilisi, and in return I grew up loving Georgia. His family sent him to America in the 90's due to the fact America was one step below paradise, and Georgia was one step above perdition at the time. I was raised during Pax Americana and had a Georgian cultural hub three houses down from mine. Looking back, it seemed inevitable I would join Peace Corps Georgia.

I was in perfect health and my professors from college, in their wisdom, suggested I join the Peace Corps. One professor, a Returned Peace Corps Volunteer herself, and the second professor, Harvard educated, made the best recommendations possible. They knew I loved America and believed that everyone should serve their country in one way or another. My professors thought my dedication and education would serve best as an English teacher and allow for me to see the world. A year after graduating with honors, I decided to apply to the Peace Corps. When I found out the Peace Corps was recruiting English teachers for Georgia, I immediately signed up. I already knew so much, and it was one of those weird moments where it seems there is some horrifying force outside of our observational powers; the stars aligned.

My want to help people has always been genuine, as I had well over three hundred hours of volunteer work before I even applied to the Peace Corps. I had been tutoring immigrants, volunteering at my local church, a veterinary clinic, and helping the world in any way I could. Now, I was going to help the people of my childhood friend. I knew beforehand, all I was there for was to teach English, help with projects, and make friends. I was an oddity; I was one of the few that knew the culture before I went in. Part of me hoped to find my long-lost friend, but that was a long shot. I received my Peace Corps invitation. I did six months of medical paperwork and was in perfect health, and had been for years. I left Ohio.

Onboard the plane heading to orientation, where all other volunteers meet up for debrief and paperwork before departure, I sat alone not knowing what to expect. It seemed like forever since my life had moved forward, it had only been two years since college and I was bored of the corporate world. Before me sat a golden opportunity. I had no idea what to expect, and resolved myself to be friendly and go with the flow. I looked back on saying goodbye to all my friends and family at the gate of the airport where we shed genuine tears. That was hard. I looked back at the year of medical paperwork, shots, vaccinations, and was happy that was done. Now I had my service to look forward to.

At the hotel, they stuck me with a guy who was by nature the modern example of a hippy. A college NGO kid with short hair and a polo shirt, did volunteer work, has experimented with drugs, and has a professional haircut: modern hippies. I met him in our hotel room in Philadelphia. We shook hands. For my part, I was more of a Catholic kid who had not missed a Sunday of Church in twenty years, who believed in the Peace Corps and helping others. I had no idea what the Peace Corps was really like, and was not prepared for the reality of it.

Three days were spent in conference. We spent eight hours a day in training seminars as they tried to prep us for the challenges to come. It was all very, very boring. A veteran of the Peace Corps said all the countries go through the same cookie cutter conferences as he had completed several tours. There were 60 volunteers in our year. We spent the days listening to the most mind-numbing lectures. The only memorable thing was watching a bizarre video where the administration tries to culture shock you through the power of cheese crackers. They made us watch a video where a bunch of government employees pretended to be in a made-up culture that revolved around women serving men cheesy crackers. They had us guess what it meant. Secret dairy worshipping cults from Wisconsin was not the correct answer.

We wanted to get this over with so we could hang out in the evenings. It was exciting as we were lumped in with a bunch of new people of the same age, and we had to find friends, and maybe the illustrious Peace Corps spouse. There is a whole romance thing about Peace Corps Volunteers finding their spouse in the Peace Corps and then having a kid, and that kid goes on to join the Peace Corps and finds a spouse. It is a hope for some. For the most part, everyone is good natured, especially in my group as we had no diplomatic wannabes, another motivation to join, money and power. Most of the people in my year were in their mid-twenties and trying to flee a boring life in the states and wanted a new and exciting adventure, in that regard, I was no different. The rest of the orientation was paperwork and everyone wanted to go to the bar afterwards.

THE BAR AFTERWARDS

We split into different groups and went to different bars. I did my usual good willed dad jokes and this group was supportive of it. These were intelligent people who knew how to laugh. The only conflict at this point was who to hang out with. The level of acceptance for humor was high with these good-natured people, and no one knew anyone. One woman my age was a fierce fighter, a very strong lady, an immigrant from Eastern Europe. She was intelligent. I would find out later she had survived a lot and overcome it all, I had respect for her. She was not the only one in this group, sadly there were many victims of similar stories. I met many volunteers who had long histories of dealing with victimization and the psychological fall out from victimization, ranging from depression and anxiety to PTSD. There were victims of rape and other atrocities.

Other volunteers were luckier, they were fleeing useless ex-husbands, monstrous boyfriends, divorces, dead end jobs, unemployment, drug addiction, and the Peace Corps accepted them all, only they looked better on paper. Only the best-looking applications are accepted. One was escaping an ex-husband who refused to do dishes, many were escaping unemployment. I was escaping a bank job; I felt I let everyone down. Not all groups were like this, this one was lucky, other volunteer groups were filled with career minded dry-water diplomats with political connections.

One night we walked around Philly. I would say it was a magical time for us, walking around and bonding with complete strangers, but I do not believe in magic. I believe in illusion. I quickly made a friend of a man named Mjolnir, tall, extremely handsome and laidback. He confided in me, "You're alright, before this I was unemployed, broke, and living on my friend's couch for 6 months." There were many like him. Great guy, really handsome.

We decided to go to a nice restaurant, then realized the prices were too high and the clientele too snobby for a group of Peace Corps Volunteers. We proceeded to a dive bar and crammed eight of us into a little corner. We blew our daily stipend on beer, nachos, and dark jokes. The night was a thousand and one jokes from people in their twenties, all unsure of themselves, apprehensive, stressed after a boring conference, and on a new adventure. We were trying to make as many friends as possible as fast as possible. It was one of those moments in time where everything seems right in the universe. We laughed ourselves stupid. Mjolnir sat there refilling my beer with the pitcher, as I caught him off-guard with a joke. A bunch of future Peace Corps Volunteers, all hopeful, sharing nachos in a cruddy little dive bar hidden in a corner of a cruddy street.

KINSHIP WITH THE DEVIL

We went back to the hotel and played small portable board games. I didn't bring any, which I still kick myself for. I made a friend of a man who had done every drug imaginable, not joking. He was in his late twenties but he looked like he was 40. I named him Druggie. A girl had led him down that road to his near destruction, we had a kinship immediately. Love lures romantics to hell. He had since cleaned up and had turned his whole life around, a monumental feat, especially knowing the stories he told me. Meth, not even once, and he kicked that habit. Think of the inhuman will to overcome the most powerful narcotic on earth. I am proud to have known him. He was a better man than I, many of them were.

    I talked literature with him, I showed him *Ambrose Bierce* and it made him laugh. It was a hoarse deep laugh. I imagine the Devil would sound like that, it was so deep and bass, when he chuckled, the universe resonated. I loved it, it was music to me. Deep and echoing, it carried. His intelligence was beyond me, he had seen the true side of humanity, and came back from the brink. I let Druggie borrow my copy of *Ambrose Bierce's The Devil's Dictionary* to read on the bus to the airport, horrifying everyone as he laughed. He handed me back the definition of peace, "Peace: A period of cheating between two periods of fighting." We laughed together.

AIRPORT

Before we even boarded the bus to the airport, one of the volunteers had food poisoning and was doubled over in the bathroom. The Peace Corps employee told him, "If you don't get on that plane, you are not going." We were all a little stunned by this, but he crawled onto the bus after wiping the vomit from his mouth. He was a tough guy, and I would consider the pinnacle of volunteers, I liked him.

I was happy for how I did my luggage. Everyone brought large bulky suitcases and were struggling; while with my one roller duffel and backpack, I sailed by with ease. I travel light, favoring mobility over comfort. Of everyone in my group, I had the most envied backpack: a 35-liter hiking backpack, perfect for size and efficiency. Going through security was easier for me. I was one of the first through. I was stopped by a TSA agent who pulled me aside, patted me down, and asked me to open my bag. I looked over at the x-ray, I had a pack of AA batteries in my backpack, they looked like bullets on the scanner. "My bad, just batteries, you can take them if you want. I'm with the Peace Corps."

He shook his head and laughed, "Nah, you see it though, right?" I thanked him for his politeness on the subject and joked with him a little bit.

I felt happy in the group. I checked the directions on the map and the gate location. I stood after the security checkpoint and directed everyone on where to go, making sure no one was left behind. The Peace Corps employee did not come with us, her job was to get us to the airport. Once everyone was through, I headed to the gate myself. Mjolnir saved me a seat. We spent the time talking and joking. I called my father to say goodbye one last time. He wished me luck, and I heard him fight back a tear over the phone, "Love you son."

"Love you too Dad." I shut down my phone and went back to Mjolnir. Airports are a turning point, once you are there, there is no going back. I told Mjolnir about my father; he gave me a hug.

A game of *Cards Against Humanity* broke out, the perfect game for Peace Corps Volunteers. We played a few hands getting to know each other. I angered a female volunteer in the best way possible. Her card was something about "what men don't know." I threw down a trap card. After looking at all the cards, she chose "the female orgasm", as she thought that was her friend's card. Her friend shook her head, and they all looked around confused. I reached my hand out and smiled. She face-palmed with a sigh of exasperation, not willing to look me in the eye. "I have not yet begun to self-deprecate!" I declared.

We boarded the plane and I was ecstatic to be placed right beside the womanizer in the group. I couldn't stand him. He moved through a couple women in the group before they realized what he was, then he switched over to using local women from the country he came to help. It was easy for him, the lure of American wealth and then using them for sex and dropping them. I heard many stories of this guy. None of them were good.

LANDING

Landing in Tbilisi, a volunteer said he saw half the city lights go out. The pilot announced we had made it and we cheered. We walked off the plane and to the luggage claim. Everyone had to wait as they had several bags to grab, except me. I had one, found, grabbed, gone. We were told to go to the next area as soon as we had our bags. I waited for the others, and I am glad I did. Had I left when I had everything, everyone else would have been ten minutes behind me. I was the first one out of the door with the others about thirty seconds behind. As I stepped out, there was a large crowd and a group of camera men. They looked confused as we looked at each other. Then they turned the cameras on me, and I smiled and walked by trying to get out of their shot. I am not one for being in the spotlight, or on national TV.

I followed the signs towards the designated waiting area as people clapped and cheered. I was confused. The rest followed me out and they were applauded and did interviews. I had no interest, although I appeared on national news. I found the waiting area and sat down on a bench with Mjolnir, we did not want any part of the limelight. We joked about it. A camera man got a shot of us and we did our best smile and wave. I was happy when the cameras left.

Everyone gathered in a group and the Country Director of Peace Corps Georgia walked out. He gave a forgettable speech and told us we were lucky to be honored by a special speaker who took time out of his busy life to greet us. Not the ambassador as he was busy, but some guy from the embassy. Here was a man with political connections, having never served in either the military or the Peace Corps, and told us how important our mission was.

HOTEL PEACE CORPS PARANOIA

We were ushered onto a bus and driven to a hotel where we received some introductory training and vaccinations, for a few days. This is where the hundreds of injections started and they kept pumping us full of vaccines. I no longer have a fear of needles. They did teach us to fear animals. The doctors spoke, "There's lots of animals on the streets, cats and dogs, do not pet them. If they break the skin by scratch or bite, come to us immediately because you will have rabies and die. Kittens have rabies and you will die. Puppies have rabies and will kill you; your brain will turn to liquid and you will die by foaming at the mouth." Everyone was in agreement; we were now afraid of puppies and kittens. Paranoia is ripe in the Peace Corps. They will teach you to fear animals, and this is not a joke, as they do carry rabies, worms, and other diseases. Americans are trained to pet animals, they had to break us of that.

The first thing the Peace Corps told us was, and I quote verbatim, "Be yourself, but don't." The Peace Corps is run on double talk and duplicity, and they are masters of it, and they will teach you how to be like them. They told us the most important thing is for the people to like you, so be yourself, but don't. This is the unofficial motto of the Peace Corps. The advice they gave was, if you are LGBTQ and in the Peace Corps, be quiet and say you have a significant other of the opposite sex, because some Georgians hate the LGBTQ community, and in Georgia, they beat them in the streets. That motto goes far beyond protecting at risk minorities though, it explains how you should think and behave, how to be a duplicitous image, how to blend in with your community when you are the foreigner. This is the truest statement in the Peace Corps, be yourself, but don't. No one is themselves in the Peace Corps, and the Peace Corps is not what it presents itself as, to foreigners and Americans alike. It is a government bureaucracy and unofficially falls under the authority of the State Department and follows their agenda, they are not an independent organization. "Be yourself, but don't" is the state of being two, the definition of duplicity.

The Peace Corps taught us the basics of life serving the government and gave us a rule book an inch thick, all about how we were to live. The constitution does not matter to the Peace Corps. To put it this way, holding a gun, like a hunting rifle your host father may hand you to examine, is enough to get you kicked out of the Peace Corps. Not firing, not fighting, just holding a gun looking at it is enough to get you kicked out of the Peace Corps. Driving a car can get you terminated. Driving a car is enough to get you kicked, and there are many more rules. Using a paper shredder or any government equipment without permission at the headquarters is a violation of the rules. If you break any of these rules, they can kick you out without a second thought. There are no rights for Peace Corps Volunteers, you have no protections, and you are not paid. You are a volunteer, and not an employee. Employees have legal protection, volunteers have nothing. All of the rules say you "should" do this or that. If you are being terminated, they give you 24 hours to quit before termination, and they always want you to quit first, it is how they maintain their image. The Peace Corps maintains an atmosphere of fear of termination to keep volunteers controlled.

A Peace Corps Volunteer from the year before told me, "Everyone is paranoid of getting kicked out, and they will kick people out over the smallest infractions. The most important thing to the Peace Corps, is the image of the Peace Corps, and they will defend it at all costs. They have kicked volunteers out unjustly because of racism, and not because the American was racist, but because the country you serve in is racist. There are racists in Georgia. An Asian-American was teaching English in her village, and the principal hated Asians, so he reported back that the volunteer was not doing their job, not coming to class, and this American was a hard worker and we all knew this person. The Peace Corps terminated her. No questions asked. Lawyers got involved. The Country Director will find a reason to kick you out if they think you are a threat to their image, and the locals' word has more weight than yours. Our first year, we were told to stay in our villages and never leave for any reason. The old Country Director was removed, they have a lot of power over our lives." This is how the Peace Corps actually functions, country directors act like dictators over their Peace Corps country.

The rule book has a lot of wording you have to pay close attention to. I would love to see a civil rights lawyers go through the book with a fine-tooth comb and see how much infringement on American rights the Peace Corps commits. The wording always said "should." You "should" do this or that or "should not." It is vague enough to give the Peace Corps a legal grey area to kick people out if it is for the convenience of the Peace Corps.

The rules state a volunteer should follow acceptable cultural sexual practices in the community they serve. This is left vague for a good reason. That is a legal mine field for the Peace Corps, and they do not want to be brought into a court room for terminating someone for having sex, or to tarnish their image. There are volunteers who have had sex with their partner teachers, their directors, and I would put money down that volunteers have had affairs with married individuals in the Peace Corps. There are all sorts of activities that occur that the Peace Corps works diligently on hiding. They will terminate volunteers for anything they deem fit, and there are no protections for a volunteer, and no appeal.

Pregnant women are not allowed in the Peace Corps. A female volunteer has two choices if she becomes pregnant while serving: abortion or termination. If a volunteer gets pregnant, the Peace Corps will kick the volunteer out for keeping the child. The Peace Corps will not be responsible for a pregnancy. When it comes to pregnancy in the Peace Corps, either the unborn is terminated or the volunteer is. The Peace Corps will pay for the abortion and get the volunteer everything they need to return to service. This is hypocrisy from the federal government. While the Supreme Court removed the right for a woman to have an abortion, they still allow it in the Peace Corps. As long as the abortion suits the needs for the federal government, it is acceptable. Unlike the US government, I believe a woman has the right to her own body. I know the crime statistics related to societies that prevent abortions.

The Peace Corps states that if a male volunteer gets a foreign woman pregnant, he "should" be responsible for the child and support it. The Peace Corps does not tell the volunteer they do not have to be responsible. There are no laws that state an American has to be a responsible father out of wedlock to a foreigner. According to US law, it is perfectly acceptable to abandon any child you conceive. No volunteer is responsible for a child in the Peace Corps. Women can get abortions or be terminated. Men can leave without supporting their child, although they will be terminated regardless of their choice in responsibility as the Peace Corps will not be responsible for any child of any volunteer male or female. Volunteers can leave pregnant women behind to fend for themselves with the burden they caused, and the US government can do nothing. This is why the rules say "should," because the Peace Corps does not want the volunteers to know the law, it is all for their image.

The funniest thing about the sexual practices of volunteers; since every volunteer has medical care and has been tested for diseases, it is essentially a giant orgy for two years, for some. In training, some groups treated it as a swinger party. The average volunteer will only have sex with other American volunteers. Only the brave or the crazy go to bed with the locals. Locals can carry HIV and HEP-C and not know it. Volunteers have contracted life threatening diseases. Oddly enough, both the female and male volunteers are curious about sex with the locals and will ask experienced volunteers what it is like, and they want details. Everyone is curious about a new type of penis or vagina. It is a scientific-diplomatic curiosity. Make love, not war, literally.

We were told we were on the job 24/7 in country. Even while we sleep, we were on the job as recognized by the US government, our country of service is our workplace. We were told, if your head is not on your official bed, you have to text your location to the government number with a government phone and you have to keep the government phone charged at all times and on you at all times. If we were not sleeping in our bed, we had to report our location every night, and they will terminate for failure to report. The only time we were allowed to not follow the rules, is when we left the country. Other than vacations, the Peace Corps controls your life. We were also told to watch the other volunteers and to report on anyone who is behaving strange or differently. Their concern is they do not want to deal with a suicide, so they told us to report on anyone who behaves odd, or is acting unusual. They wanted us to report on each other. I turned to the friends I made and told them, "If you have problems, you call me." They nodded and thanked me.

Volunteers from the previous year taught us the unofficial reality. We learned sexual harassment is guaranteed for all women, sexual assault is frequent and goes unreported, and so many crimes go unreported. Georgian men have exposed their genitals to female volunteers, because they see American media and think all American women are whores. Volunteers from the year before us told us that the Peace Corps does not want to deal with reports. One volunteer from the year before us, told us how he was mugged by a taxi driver over three dollars. He was slammed against a car and he told us, "Just give them the money and walk away, don't report it, you have to be a bitch in the Peace Corps sometimes. You have to suck it up." Volunteers who are not white, have to deal with being called racial slurs, and asked what country they were really from, all from the people they came to help. The best advice we received was from a black volunteer, as he said, "stand better than them, if they call you anything, turn and say good morning or hello, show strength in face of their ignorance." Racism is rampant, and that is the one thing America does not have a monopoly on.

Crime between Peace Corps Volunteers is the biggest thing that goes unreported, and we were suggested to not report anything. The Peace Corps strongly suggested to report crimes without names to a special reporting system that only shows statistics, but does not do any criminal prosecution. The best example of this unwritten rule, is the case of

Deborah Gardner, who was murdered by a male volunteer while serving. The Peace Corps and the US government actively aided and abetted the murderer and helped him get away with his crime. Deborah Gardner was stabbed 22 times for refusing to have sex. One of the main priorities of Peace Corps Georgia is teaching feminism. The Peace Corps only acts legally to protect itself. The Peace Corps has no interest in protecting their volunteers outside of Peace Corps image. This is the golden rule of the Peace Corps: The Peace Corps image is more important than the volunteer.

Then we were told that everything we do will be watched by the locals and they will gossip about us. Which is true, and everyone watches the volunteers like a hawk. It is rather unnerving, but you get used to it, and then bored and annoyed by the stupid stories they gossip about. Everyone watches you in the Peace Corps. Other volunteers from the year before told us not to screw around in our village as that will get you fired. You are here as images of the US people and you are here to show the US People can be trusted, that is it.

DON'T ASK, DON'T TELL

I heard a Peace Corps government employee state there were no volunteers with psychological issues in the Peace Corps. That person was so nice looking and professional, I missed the blatant lie. The Peace Corps demands that you put down your psychological history in the application. It is an automatic rejection if you put anything down, every volunteer knows this, not every applicant does. If you want to be a volunteer, write nothing, say nothing.

The Peace Corps "Don't Ask, Don't Tell" policy has nothing to do with being gay, as the Peace Corps does not care about your sexual orientation. The new "Don't Ask, Don't Tell" policy concerns people with mental health issues or a history of mental health issues. The Peace Corps does not accept people with mental health problems in the Peace Corps if it is on the application. I have met volunteers with histories of mental health problems, and did they write it down on their application? No, because they would never get in. The Peace Corps itself will instruct you on privacy laws for health issues, and tell you to be quiet or you give up your legal protection. They will tell you to never tell anyone anything about your medical history, as that waives your right to privacy. If they find out you had a mental health problem at any time in your life and did not write it down, they will kick you out of the Peace Corps and you will be banned for life. This is official policy. The Corps of the Peace Corps the only accurate part of the name. It is a diplomatic corps, nothing more.

The Peace Corps persecutes people with mental health problems in the exact same way the US Military did in the 90's with members of the LGBTQ+ community. This is how they operate to avoid any legal situations. There is no support for mental health issues in the Peace Corps. They may say they care, but not enough to change anything or actually help people with psychological issues, even stemming from abusive Peace Corps Country Directors. At the time of writing, they are being sued over denying an applicant who had depression. I have met volunteers with PTSD, rape survivors who joined the Peace Corps, volunteers with anxiety, depression, and anything you can think of. I have met them all in the Peace Corps and they are there. None of them wrote anything down on their application. I received a stress disorder from the Peace Corps myself, and was abused by a Country Director after almost being killed. They do not want to hear about your psychological health and do not care about your mental health, only the image matters. If they find out anything about it, they will kick you out.

You can look up reports and interviews about the lack of mental health care in the Peace Corps and post service, there are a lot of them. Why is this taboo? Because it costs money to fix the problem. The Peace Corps wants to present itself as open minded and progressive, do not believe it. When it comes to mental health, they terminate volunteers and alienate people who are victims. Be yourself, but don't. The Peace Corps can get more volunteers.

When you are in the Peace Corps, if you have psychological problems, they tell you to call the doctors and speak with them. If the doctors have time, they will listen if you call, but for my country, it was two doctors covering 120+ people night and day. If they have time, they can help, if not, it is your problem. They want you to create your own support network and not depend on them. Here is the other problem. The doctors can send you home if they think you represent a threat to your health or others, or if they cannot provide adequate care in country, or if they discovered you have a past history of mental health. If you say the word suicide, you are going home immediately. You cannot talk to these people psychologically without risking medical termination. It is a trap, and only the doctors will decide what to do with you. There is no appeal.

Every volunteer is afraid or at least aware of the fact that psychological help in the Peace Corps is not to be trusted. The Country Director of Georgia tried to implement a program of volunteers supporting volunteers psychologically, but there was no confidentiality and no legal protections. How does this help? The solution for the Peace Corps bureaucracy is simple, kick them out and get a new volunteer. The Peace Corps does not care about the volunteers with psychological issues. On paper they do, because if you have issues, they kick you out, and you are no longer a volunteer, and thus no volunteers have psychological issues. The US government has you for two years, they do not want to take care of you the rest of your life. It isn't profitable.

REST OF PRE- PRE- SERVICE TRAINING

The stress was high. During break, I can remember looking out the window, at the town. Rusted pipes and old buildings, decaying and crumbling infrastructure, cracked cement. It felt gritty and real. I sat there looking at graffiti in a foreign language. Druggie came over, "We're in it now." I smiled with him, he put his arm around me. We looked at the peaceful decay outside, the post-soviet country, Georgia.

The government covered other administrative procedures. They gave us our government issued phones, which were the cheapest phones imaginable. *Nokia* bricks, but they had the old games like *Bubble Shooter* and *Snake*. They told us to keep lots of condoms with us at all times, as volunteers have caught HIV, HEPC, and green card wives. Everyone is given twenty condoms to start and then you can get more for free.

We were interviewed by the program managers who were all local Georgians. They asked why we wanted to come to Georgia. They were not prepared for my answer. "I came here to learn more about my childhood friend's culture and homeland. My best friend was from Tbilisi." They were shocked, never had they heard that before. "He was a good man." I could read the concern on the Georgians' faces at the mention of the word "was". "I lost contact with him. Maybe I'll find him here."

The sympathy was genuine, and so were my intentions. I grew up with Georgian culture and missed it. He was my first foreign friend in the third grade. It was part of why I came here. I was searching for the something I had lost long ago. Every day we were together, walking to school. They wished me luck and never asked me another question. Most of the answers were to try something new, help the world, travel, learn, and all the basics. I was a little different, this service meant something deeply important.

MISSION INTEGRITY

Several officials from the embassy come to our program to assure us the Russians would not invade. There was something I noticed. While another embassy person was talking to the group, the Country Director and the security specialist were speaking off to the side in a jovial manner, like they had been friends for years and were making small jokes. The Country Director removed his Peace Corps Georgia lapel pin and handed it to the security specialist who put it on his lapel. It is as easy as that, wearing a pin and you become Peace Corps. The security expert told us to avoid strip clubs and other seedy places as they are run by the Georgian mafia.

Later the Country Director, the head of the US Peace Corps program in Georgia, the highest-ranking Peace Corps Official and government officer here, told us: "We are here to string Georgia along to NATO. It's better for them as they develop and move forward little by little." He literally said the Peace Corps' goal in Eastern Europe was to string countries along towards NATO, so the Peace Corps had a military objective. I had to double check and see other Peace Corps programs in Eastern Europe. Sure enough, ever since the fall of the USSR, the Peace Corps was the first one in. Ever since the fall, the Peace Corps has been moving further east preparing those former soviet countries to join NATO. Poland in the 90's, now NATO. There are many more. The Peace Corps in Eastern Europe is politically motivated to spread America's military agenda. The Peace Corps says it is not political, what they mean is they do not care about democrats or republicans. Wherever the Peace Corps goes, it serves America's political agenda, and it can range from simple public relations and foreign aid in Africa to fostering the expansion of military alliances in Eastern Europe. The Peace Corps is a political multi-purpose tool.

Our job was to convince the conservative population of Georgia to move towards America. I felt unsure of myself after this. The Peace Corps says they are not political, but why this? This explains why the Peace Corps is in eastern Europe. The Peace Corps usually uses an economic index for developing countries, most of Europe, including Georgia was well above the cut off line. The Peace Corps came to Georgia to sway public opinion; soft diplomacy if you like technical terms. We were told repeatedly to teach Western ideals, feminism, and to CONQUER the hearts and minds of everyone we come into contact with. They taught us to respect the other culture, but at the same time, to teach their children to be more American, to spread American ideals in the country. The Peace Corps subtly teaches that American culture is superior, and there is an atmosphere of American superiority in the Peace Corps. They jokingly told us to violate the prime directive from *Star Trek*. I and several other volunteers become uncomfortable with this.

PRE-SERVICE TRAINING

SINK OR SWIM

Perhaps the saddest part was when we were split into small groups to learn Georgian. Mjolnir, Druggie, and I were separated. We reached out to each other as we were being pulled away, staring into each other's eyes. I was stuck with volunteers I did not know. Our group was then bussed to Gori, birthplace of Stalin. The man who ruled the Soviet Union was Georgian and Gori worships him as a demigod, you have to see it, it feels like it is out of a *Bond* movie. There was six of us in my class and we spent the next three months together, day in, day out, six days a week, nine hours a day, learning Georgian and whatever else we needed. We were dropped off in the center of town to meet our host families. We stood in the middle of a park under a statue of Stalin and our names were called to us and we were sent to our respective families. I was quiet, I shook hands, and said hello. I never expected to see a statue of Stalin in the Peace Corps.

FIRST MONTH

The first month was mental anguish. It is sink or swim in training, and I was sinking in the beginning. Nine hours a day of training, intense hardcore training for six days a week for three months straight. The best phrase to tell yourself in training is, "I'll get through it, it ain't gonna be pretty, but I'll get through it". I did not come out of my room for the first couple weeks, only slowly coming out and seeing everyone for a little bit at a time. I was exhausted all the time, and mentally drained. By the end of a normal day, I was so crammed full of information, all I could do was sit, and then I had homework. My hair started falling out and I woke up with my pillow covered in hair. I did not have any friends in the group at the start. Half the group only gossiped about other groups, and talked trash. When I asked to cut out the gossiping, they said it was good for socializing, and all they were doing was bad mouthing others. Most of my problems came from the Americans I was with, as the designated leader of the group was nothing but a pushy control freak who gossiped. I had to tell her to not give me orders. I stuck to the Georgian family I was with.

I was overstressed and training is built that way. Everyone is stressed, in intestinal pain, and trainees fight and argue over anything. Everyone is miserable. My first month they had to take me to the emergency room which is nerve wracking, and if I would be sent back or allowed to stay.

Being sick and having trouble breathing, surrounded by foreigners in a foreign country, what a baptism. I was scared, I was afraid I would be sent home. I was coughing up green and all sorts of colors. It is scary as hell being overseas, knowing no one and needing medical help. I became so stressed I ended up with a lung infection and a fever. I had to rest for a week in the Georgian doctor's care which was a very small hotel. I slept for a week which was the happiest part of training for me. It was the only break I had during training, and I was so thankful for it. Then again it took a moderate lung infection to get me to rest. Good did come of it, I had to give up caring and focus on surviving, which is a good way to think.

A FISH OUT OF WATER

My host father was a former soviet officer, spoke multiple languages including German, and was a radio communications specialist. I knew what he was doing during the Cold War, he was spying on foreign communications. I had seen his decorations, his medals, and the awards he had been given, he was heavily decorated. His uniform was odd. He was some sort of Soviet State Police Officer. If the USSR continued, I have no doubt he would have been a director, or some other high-ranking position. I respected him, but I knew I was an American kid to him. He was a stern and austere man, tall, lean, and had a winter beaten face. He held himself as grandfatherly stoic. He communicated cleanly and clearly in curt orders when dealing with me. "Dajecki, Adecki, Modi", he said as if in a military canine unit, sit, stand, come. He was intelligent, I could see it in his eyes. H wanted to help his country, so he welcomed an American volunteer into his home and helped prepare him for his service. I was humbled.

My host father understood complex issues easily, and could read me like a map. I imagine being in a security force trained him on how to read others. He spoke and had the mannerisms of my grandfather. I found it funny how soldiers on opposite sides of geopolitical issues have much in common. You could switch out beer for wine and he was the same familial joker as my blue-collar grandpa, only more stoic in the east bloc way. He was not a heavy drinker. This was one of the smartest men I had ever met, luckily, he was an honest man. His language skills were flawless. Never underestimate a Georgian, they might not have the cash, but they have the intelligence, and they are quiet about it.

I went to Church with his family multiple times, there are few differences between Catholicism and Eastern Orthodox. I spent the evenings with his family in the living room as he read and I studied. He told me once in Georgian, "I know your type, you will go to Tbilisi one day, and you will find a wife, one of our girls, not an American." On occasion he helped me with my studies. For him everything was mathematically broken down. He knew how to connect our cultures through mutual likes. One evening we sat together and watched one of the greatest movies I have ever seen: *Soldier's Father* in English, or *Jariskatsis Mama* if you know Georgian. This movie left me slack jawed, but it opened my eyes to foreign movies. I followed the movie without knowing much of the language. This is where I fell in love with the Georgian language.

The outside of their house was flat and grey, a two-story house on a quiet little street in a small town. The inside was gorgeous. I have been in million-dollar houses that looked cheap compared to this. The house was furnished like an old university library. The floor was a deep brown oak and covered with a red rug. The walls were lined with rows of bookshelves. I climbed a curved stair case to ascend to my room through a double door. I had a desk and a bed with an old soviet mattress, and it was obviously a guest room. My balcony looked out over a cramped but expertly manicured garden. I sat in the garden and wrote on my day off, trying to process with an over-loaded and over stressed brain from all the Georgian.

FAMILY

The mother was a little old woman. Every morning she set oatmeal and a hard-boiled egg for me on the table. I had two host brothers who were my age. One would constantly fight and yell every night the first month, loud fights when he was drunk. I had to ask my teacher about it, as he was fighting every night, I could not help but stay away and lock myself in my room as I did not want to deal with a drunk. He wanted me to drink with him all the time. I stopped drinking during training, except if my Soviet father wanted to, which was rare. After about a month, the older brother left, as I suspect my teacher said something to his mother and he was given the boot temporarily. I suspect he had PTSD from the 2008 war.

I was closer with my other host brother and he reminded me of my childhood friend. He was an athlete, a top notch one. He had injured his leg long ago, but he did not let that stop him. We shared a similar injury. I had extensive surgery on my knee as a teenager due to a football injury. I showed him how to stretch it properly and how to keep it flexible and his knee felt better after his exercises. I carried the physical therapists training with me. He thanked me for it. The first time I had a brother was in the Georgia. We worked out together in his makeshift gym. On one event he put too many weights on me and my arms gave out, and I yelled "help" in Georgian and he grabbed them off of me, we laughed. I had not realized how weak I had become.

He lived in his parents' home which was common. He and I joked and lived as brothers. He gave me my first hair cut in Georgia. He spent an hour cutting my hair with this old janky soviet trimmer, and I had a buzz cut by the end of it. We spent the evening cutting my hair as it was incredibly thick. I had the Georgian summer cut that all professional men get in late spring. I could not complain, it was free and refreshing. We took photos as he sheared me, then he sheared his father. He was the family barber.

The next day was a large group conference where the Country Director of Peace Corps Georgia publicly yelled at me for my hair cut, he was angry, "What are you doing? Joining the Georgian cadets, if you want in the Georgian military get out of my Peace Corps!"

I said in a calm and composed voice, "My host brother gave me this haircut last night. We made an evening out of cutting my hair and his father's, it was a family event."

To drive the point home, my Georgian teacher came over and started examining my hair with all smiles as she made me turn my head to examine it, she said loudly, "Oh, I love your Georgian haircut, you are one of us now. Your brother did a wonderful job." The Country Director walked away pretending to check his phone. It is all an image with these people. He was abusive and I was not even sworn in yet.

I was yelled at for doing my job perfectly. I was proving successful at adapting and living with the locals, and I had not even left training. I had a personal reason to love this country. It was a paycheck and status for him. This was my first encounter with the Country Director, he would be like this every time I met him. I later found out he introduced military traditions into the Peace Corps, like a Peace Corps challenge coin. If you know what challenge coins are, you know how worthless a Peace Corps Volunteer challenge coin is. Why was he harping on me for a haircut? The Country Director was always dodging questions. When a trainee asked about medical care being denied post service and the problems associated with the Peace Corps, he said it was covered and walked away. If there is one thing you learn in the Peace Corps, the government is only good at walking away. Genuine people will find unexpected difficulties in the Peace Corps

FREE TABLE AND FAMILY BONDING

Back at Peace Corps HQ, in the capital, there was a free table where volunteers put clothes and valuable items they did not want, but another volunteer could use. Even though I was not supposed to, I took clothes for my family, like sports shirts. My host brother was ecstatic when I gave him an *Under Armour* shirt. He called his friends over and they all tried it on. He loved it. I found many items I gave to my friends. I even taught my host father's grandchild a little English. My host family reported to my teacher on how I was progressing. They found it funny how I slowly came out of my room, like a groundhog checking to see if it was safe. Midway through training they asked my teacher if they could keep me for the two years. We were all disappointed.

I had to ask my teacher about my host brother. "Is it normal for a guy in his mid-twenties to date a sixteen-year-old girl?" She said no, but I got the distinct feeling she was saving face. This is village life, and you have to learn what to question and what not to. She was a friendly girl, and his parents dubbed them Romeo and Juliet. They ended up having a healthy relationship all things considered. As a guest and friend, I wish them a prosperous future, and it is not my place to judge.

We all had dinner together and I bought a nice bottle of wine for everyone. My host father ignored my gift and cracked open the most delicious cognac I had ever had. It was the smoothest liquor ever to hit my tongue. He laughed at the look on my face when I took a sip and drank slowly. I rarely drank in the Peace Corps, but that was good homemade cognac. I approached experiences in the Peace Corps slowly. In comparison, the Country Director openly encouraged getting drunk with the locals. I passed on that as fights broke out with the American male trainees.

LANGUAGE TRAINING

It is stressful, everyone is exhausted and having health problems. Everyone has diarrhea in the Peace Corps. Every few weeks it seemed like I had a mild case of food poisoning. I threw up a lot. Everyone deals with this. I kept toilet paper in my bag in case I had to jump behind a bush. Despite it all, I learned to get by. I did the best I could in class given the circumstances. I attended tutoring after class to improve my language skills.

You have to find something to look forward to everyday. Every day I felt brain dead and exhausted. My hair was falling out. I was dealing with health issues and stress in a foreign environment. I was stuck wearing the same unwashed clothes, studying Georgian grammar six days a week in summer, in an unairconditioned school. Every day I looked forward to one thing. During any break I could, I sat in the window of the classroom, and looked out on verdant hills of Gori. The one peaceful moment I had was looking out on the hills, and thinking how beautiful the country side looked in the sun. That was a moment out of time for me. In all stress and chaos, I could sit and reflect on what a beautiful country I found myself in. It was only for five minutes.

MS. LISA

For the first month she remained quiet and observing, and only by joking did we find each other after the first month. She lived next door and we became comrades in tongues as we learned Georgian together. Every morning I would wait for her at the corner, or vice versa, and we walked to school together, no matter the morning weather. We walked a mile every day to school, joking all along the way. We were ready for another mind-numbing adventure. We shared many commonalities. She taught me much and opened my mind to different ways of seeing the world. She was well educated in international affairs and preached realpolitik. She questioned what it meant to be morally good. I believe she grew annoyed with my own blind patriotism and questioned me.

We spent the few evenings we had together. We went to her house or mine, my host father loved her. We watched football on the TV and passed out together on the ancient couch, exhausted from the day's work. Other times we watched old cartoons from our childhood and reminisced about the 90's, a favorite hobby of millennials. Many nights we listened to *Eminem* and talked about how he had to fight with the government to merely sing. We became close and studied together. She often asked for my help in translating quotes from Latin, my second language. When she came across the phrase "the best days go first", we found a grim millennial reality.

REST OF TRAINING

We were all looking forward to moving on with our service. I butted heads with an overbearing trainee who I had to tell not to micromanage me. She never listened and had the Peace Corps savior complex some volunteers develop. I did not like being part of that group. We were working on some project for the week and she wanted to spend every single free moment working on the project. I wanted to see my friend Mjolnir who I rarely saw anymore, to her dismay. I overheard her reporting on me to a Georgian manager, "He's not helping."

His reply was hilarious, "Have you asked?" She had no answer then left. When she did ask me, I handed her the finished project.

She was shocked, "How? When?"

"I finished it on the first day, I work faster on my own." That was the point she backed off. Truth be told, some people work better on their own. I could never get a word in edge wise and all my suggestions were ignored. Why bother working hard for someone when they have no respect for you? Once she backed off, our relationship evened out. Oddly enough, we became dance partners when we had to take Georgian dance lessons. We called each other our "arch-nemesis and dance partner."

I was successful with the locals as all the Georgians only said positive comments about me. My slow approach the first month allowed me to take cautious steps and gave me a moment to relearn how to live from the locals and adopt their customs. Other Americans dived right in and were getting drunk and causing fights. Volunteers could not hold their drink in the birthplace of wine and became belligerent. Slurs were thrown around. I typically stayed home with the Georgians, but I heard the stories. We were all given the talk as a group as an official report had to be filed. The official ignored me as the Georgians were asking for me to stay. I helped with chores, taught their children, and lived with them. Idiots were picking fights in the Peace Corps.

OUR ONE TRIP

We were allowed to spend a night at a friend's house once in training. I went out with Mjolnir. We spent the evening hiking and watching the sunset over the Georgian countryside. He gave me the best compliment I have ever been given, "You're the type of guy I'd love to do shrooms with."

I smiled, "That's the nicest thing anyone's ever said to me." I hope the offer still stands. Only idiots do drugs in the Peace Corps. Even people who use drugs regularly are afraid to do anything while serving.

We joked about the new Peace Corps emblem while watching the sunset. The old Peace Corps emblem was simple, an American flag with stars transforming into a dove. The new emblem looked like a pigeon pooping out the American flag like it had diarrhea. It looked cheap. I dubbed it "The Shittin' Pigeon". My friend burst out laughing at the name, he agreed in laughter. The Peace Corps administration stated they needed something new and clickable for the age of smartphones. Mjolnir said it looked like a unicorn if you turned the symbol upside down, with the beak acting as the horn, and the flag as the unicorn's mane. We all liked the old one better.

We bunked together in his huge bedroom. It was two beds shoved together so we took sides. We lay there in shorts and shirts, talking. We could hear the rats in the rafters. He joked, "One night I heard a rat fall inside the wall and it spent the entire night climbing back up."

I laughed, "That rat gave me hope. You can do it buddy, climb back to your rat family and rat friends, climb, climb. One paw in front of the other my diseased friend!" We cheered for the rats; we were emotionally supporting rats. I was an expert. It was a chill evening and a welcome break from the chaos. He talked about the family he lived with and how they liked him better than the previous year's group. That group did nothing but each other for three months straight. Not every year is the same.

FRAT ALTRUISM

One day during conference, the Country Director had all the men stand up, had us raise our right hand, and vow in public, "I will not have sex with anyone under the age of 18." We all looked at each other confused. There are in hushed tones, rumors spoken about what volunteers have done. The fact a high-ranking US government official had us all stand up and take an oath, means that a volunteer in the Peace Corps has had sex with a minor. I have spoken with volunteers from other countries, and they have nodded in disgust when I asked about it. I do not know of any statistics because that is one number the Peace Corps will avoid like the plague. The Peace Corps serves in countries that do not care about girls as much, where forced under age marriages occur and even bride napping. Georgia is one of them.

Every year, one group of Americans goes in, one group goes out. Each group is different. Our group was a bunch of people trying to get away from something, for the most part, all good people. The previous year was filled with politically connected volunteers who joined to get a job with the state department. They acted like a high school clique. Even members of their own year said how it was a frat party. The group the year before us called my year "whiners". One of their own turned and told us, "At least you have the courage to state what is wrong." I liked him.

Every trainee had to spend a night and a day with a volunteer from the previous year and see what life as a volunteer was like. I was stuck with the Jock of my year, and we were sent to the middle of Georgia to the site of the volunteer we were to live with. It was a waste of time and taxpayer dollars. The volunteer from the previous year taught us nothing. He was a credit to the Peace Corps Volunteers who join up only to get a job with the State Department after service as his family was politically connected. He sat on a committee of a large well-known project and buddied up to the Country Director. He knew how charm and talk confidently; he acted like a politician. His language did not work on me, so he focused on the Jock. I will never forget the first things he said to us, "If you want to get laid, call Sally from our year, she's a slut and will fuck anybody." One of the main goals of Peace Corps Georgia is to spread feminism and gender equality. He was declared a success by the Peace Corps and went on to work with USAID. In Georgia, USAID focuses on improving gender equality.

A life of wealth and leisure on the tax payers' dollar was his destiny. He joined the Peace Corps to get into the Foreign Service. This is another reason the Peace Corps exists. America is an isolated country, and we are terrible with languages and foreign relations. The Peace Corps is a solution; it is two years of intense training in a foreign country where you have to adapt and learn and convince foreigners to like you. The Peace Corps is a system that changes college kids into diplomats to serve in the ranks of the Foreign Service, USAID, or even the CIA. You have to wait a few years for the CIA. If you have connections to the Foreign Service, if you join the Peace Corps, it is essentially a free ticket in. There is a monetary reward for joining the Peace Corps. This Frat Boy clearly hated his service, looked down on the locals, spoke negatively about the Georgians, and was doing it for the future pay check. He was elitest, and looked down on everyone, and if ever questioned, he turned acidic. He only referred to women in his year as sluts.

That night, the Frat Boy managed to get the Jock vomiting drunk. He took sadistic joy in hurting him. This was fraternity style hazing, Peace Corps hazing. I disappointed him. He hoped to harm us all but succeeded only in harming the Jock. Throughout the night, he tried to force us to drink more than the local custom. This was a premeditated strike. Even his host father questioned him on the amount he tried to force on us, a big red flag for a Georgian. The Georgian refused to drink the amount pushed on us. His host father told him to slow down. He ignored his host father, and broke custom.

I watched him pour glass after glass to the brim in the Jock's glass, while for his own he poured half a glass, and only sipped and told us to drink the whole glass. I drank at a reduced speed and took small sips. Georgians are fine when it comes to teaching foreigners their customs as long as you support their culture. The Frat Boy tried manipulating me on it, saying "You are not a man. You have to drink the full glass." I ignored him. He was pouring the drinks faster than the local custom. He forced the Jock to drink full glasses of wine like shots. I paid attention to his host father and followed the Georgian's lead who was drinking at a significantly slower rate and following custom. The Frat's host father poured the normal amount. Georgians will not betray their customs when it comes to wine. This Peace Corps Volunteer was disgracing it in the name of hazing.

When the Frat Boy accused me of insulting the culture, I asked his host father in Georgian about the speed of my drinking, he said "No Problem." I starred the Frat Boy down and he backed off and focused his attention on the Jock. The Jock went along with the Frat boy's hazing, despite my warnings. The Jock became stumbling drunk, and was blacking out. I helped the Jock to the outhouse to throw up, carrying him on my shoulder. He could barely walk. He closed the door on me. He acknowledged he was ok. The Frat Boy did nothing to help.

When I walked back from the outhouse, the Frat asked with a sickening grin from the balcony, looking down on me, "Did he throw up?" I shook my head saying I didn't know. The Frat looked disappointed. He wanted to get the Jock vomiting drunk on purpose, and he wanted to enjoy it. He asked me again, same answer. He kept asking me. His smile gave away the fact he was not concerned for the Jock's health. I held my wine and quit early which seemed to anger the Frat Boy more than anything. I checked on the Jock, he got it out of his system. The Frat Boy wanted to get us stumbling drunk and make us look like fools for his own pleasure; I doubted his sincerity from the start. This was a Peace Corps Volunteer.

There are good volunteers in the Peace Corps, but there are volunteers who will do anything to get ahead. For the Frat Boy, the Peace Corps was a hurdle for a government job. The Jock ended up fine after I got him some water and put him to bed and cleaned up. An honest volunteer from the year before told me they were trying to get as many of the new volunteers as vomiting drunk as possible in a hazing game, and that was why they signed up to mentor trainees. Yes, there are frat boys and hazing rituals in the Peace Corps. He was trying to harm us. I never expected schadenfreude in the Peace Corps, but there it is, a Peace Corps success story.

The same honest volunteer told us about another game they played. A group of male volunteers of his year rated all the new female volunteers from my year on how "fuckable" each of the women were and had a rating system. We came here to help spread gender equality, feminism, and these volunteers were the living embodiment of objectification. They were on committees and in positions of leadership to "help" the incoming volunteers. When the new female volunteers came in, these Peace Corps men began ranking how "fuckable" each woman was based on their photo. This was the leadership of the Peace Corps Volunteers from previous year in Georgia. They were frat boys with connections. All while working for the US government on the taxpayer's dollar. Forget altruism. The Peace Corps is only foreign aid and a diplomatic training ground.

The women of their year were not any better. For one committee, the female volunteers only chose the cutest boys from my year to work with. At one point I visited the HQ. A woman of Frat Boy's year asked me to take a photo of her and her friends while they were working on some project. I had my digital camera and was working on the settings when she yelled at me for taking too long, "Are you going to take the damn picture?" I was adjusting my camera. Her eyes instantly went wide as she realized her social mistake and made a fake apology, "I'm so sorry, oh my god!" Her personality shifted to playing emotional weakness as she clapped her hands over her mouth like she didn't know what she was saying. It is only an image with these people, the perfect Peace Corps Volunteers. She had the same career path as the Frat Boy. I noticed these types only did projects with name recognition. I was disillusioned.

GEORGIAN SIDE

The most important thing in the Peace Corps is how much the locals like you. If they like you, you are in. The Georgian staff of the Peace Corps liked me. They loved having me around to the point they gave me the answers for the test on government reporting. I passed everything else on my own with flying colors. There are several tests you have to pass to become a volunteer. Language is the most important, and no one helps you.

I chatted with all the locals I could and for me, it was like talking to my childhood friend, and I got along well with all of them. I asked them if they wanted me to point out any grammatical errors in their speech and they all said yes. They came to me for questions on English, and I explained correct usage of idioms and other grammatical issues. The word "the" is the hardest for any nonnative speaker. Every now and then I caught an error and broke it down for them. I praised them for their efforts. All of the Georgian managers had to work to hard get where they are. One teacher had to memorize an entire chapter of James Joyce and recite it flawlessly word for word to get her degree. I had the group applaud her for her efforts. She blushed.

STEALING HEARTS AND SAYING GOODBYE

My job was simple, my gun was my smile, and I was trigger happy. You learn the Peace Corps smile. We were the proud shining faces of America. Your job is to make people think highly of America. The day came when we passed our tests and we were given our assignment for the next two years. The assignment letter was covered with images from *Dr. Seuss's All the Places You'll Go*. The Peace Corps is obsessed with this book. We were paired with our principals and directors. My principal was a quiet woman who had a school in Adjara, near Batumi, and that was my home for my tour.

My principal called back to her village and told my future partner teacher that they were getting a white man in his mid-twenties. My future partner teacher told all the female high school students to be good because, "he is wealthy and might marry you and take you to America." I face palmed when I heard this. Then I heard about a Peace Corps Volunteer from a few years before, who served in the same village. She had married an 18-year-old boy from the village and ran off to America with him. The volunteer was 30 and her husband was 18. Good for them, they have a healthy happy relationship, and honestly, it is refreshing to hear women going after 18-year-olds. I am a feminist if anything.

After the main meeting was over, I gathered all the pencils, pens, and notepads laying around. I filled my backpack with school supplies and gave them to my partner teacher. My principal approved of my pilfering, calling me resourceful. Those schools have little. They had two computers in the school that had the combined power of a modern pregnancy test.

All Peace Corps Volunteers steal, especially from hotels. I stole the least; I took all the shampoo, coffee, and tea I could. Sometimes taking a box from the storage closets. I gave them away to locals and other volunteers, call me the Peace Corps Robin Hood. Other volunteers stole pillows, robes, bedsheets, anything that was not bolted down. The hotels are paid nicely by the government. I ripped off the free drinks, I was not taking chattel. One woman was shoving pillows into her suitcase when I walked in and said to me "Don't judge, I'm living on a mountain, I deserve comfort." I did not judge her.

The nights in the hotels were nice, everyone went swimming after dinner. After getting out of the pool, I was about to board an elevator when I farted and realized it was more than a fart. I turned around and clench-ran to the locker room to clean up. Thank Jesus it was not in the pool. Mjolnir laughed at the story, "yeah I pooped myself in a bar one night, ruined the evening, had to throw my underwear in the trash." We laughed ourselves to sleep. It was a nice resort. The policy changed after that event as a resort was not in line with the Peace Corps image.

The hardest part was saying goodbye. I had to leave my host family. Leaving families is a job requirement in the Peace Corps. I rushed down to buy wine, chocolates, and tea for my host family as a thank you. We ate and toasted. They were a Georgian family I grew to love and respect. I had a job to do, and I said goodbye. The mountains and rivers of Adjara awaited. Lisa was assigned to the other side of the country. We spent the last night of training together watching football and passed out on the couch.

SWEARING IN

Only three people did not make it, one for medical, one for quitting, and one the Country Director refused to allow in as a volunteer. The Country Director told us, "It's now on you to serve. When you take your oath, raise your right hand, if you raise your left, I am kicking you out." Apparently, it was a joke that had to do with Russian spies. I didn't get the joke. I did not trust him. He never allowed a natural photo to be taken of him, even when he was talking with Lisa in front of the American flag at the swearing in ceremony. The last conversation I had with the Country Director while in training, was about mold. I visited my village where I would be serving for the next two years. My room was covered in black mold. I asked the Country Director, "My room is covered in black mold, any ideas on how to get rid of it?"

He said with a knowing smile, "The goal is to contain; containment is the objective." I was confused at the time. Was he trying to clue me in on some diplomatic tactic, or was he quoting from the secret book of Peace Corps Directors on how to keep problems from spreading? I know now, that the policy the US government uses for controlling foreign powers is to contain their influence. For example, spreading NATO further east to contain Russian influence, as that is the objective of all US programs in Eastern Europe, including the Peace Corps. It is all to stop Russia from ever coming back. The same policy exists for China. I have no idea why he was saying this at the swearing in ceremony, but his solution was useless for dealing with mold. He did reveal how he thought; he contained problems, captured them, and kept them stuck in place.

One highly logical volunteer said it best, "bleach, kills everything." The conversation ended. I was officially serving the American government as a Peace Corps Volunteer. I was happier to be done with training, as everyone was.

SERVICE

AN OVERWHELMING SENSELESS ADVENTURE

My new host father looked like he stepped out of *Animal Farm*. I rode with him to my new home. He drove his friend's car, which was a tiny Soviet econobox. I was cramped in there for eight hours, but happy to be riding in something other than a Marshutka for once. My tiny village was an hour from Batumi. At night we drove through the dazzling city lights of the port city. We took one turn and found ourselves in total darkness as we moved onto the mountain road beyond. We drove through the mountains and pulled up in front of a dilapidated Soviet apartment block with crumbling steps. I dragged my suitcase up to my new family's apartment and into my new room, which was the size of a guest bathroom. They cleaned up the room and there was no more mold. It was a tiny room, had a small bed, small desk, and a small wardrobe. I threw everything down.

We proceeded to eat as they folded out a table and filled it with sausages and Georgian foods I cannot spell. The apartment was a small kitchen, living room, and 3-bedroom affair with a closet for a bathroom. I had two host brothers, a host mother, and a host father. I turned in due to the mental exhaustion of change. It was odd, I could not feel. I was mentally over stimulated. I passed out.

I woke up and heard rushing water. I thought someone left the sink on. Then I looked out the window at the small waterfall behind the apartment building. I never lived near a waterfall before. My room overlooked my new school, but as it was summer, it was closed. The first thing I did was clean my room. I organized the wardrobe in the most efficient way possible and used the ceiling space to hold up towels and coats. The room was cramped. I spent weeks trying to find coat hangers. I was so happy when I found them, it was like opening a chest in *The Legend of Zelda*. The mosquitos and bugs were swarming everywhere in the humid summer heat. I had to smack them off me constantly. I was covered in bug bites all summer, and woke up many times with mosquitos on my face.

Breakfast was bread and jam, simple foods. I got up and put on my shoes and walked outside in shorts and a t-shirt. There were around two hundred people in the village. It was a rural river mountain valley. There were more cows than people, creepy mountain cows. You could look up and see ten tons of beef grazing on the side of a mountain; it was not natural for an Ohioan. They acted like mountain goats; it was disturbing to see. I was worried about a beef-slide if the cows came tumbling down.

FIRST STEP

The most serene feeling from serving is your first day in your village or site. You wake up, excited, not knowing anything, and you have to explore. Once training is over, the Peace Corps throws you out into the middle of nowhere and says good luck for the next two years. It is a magical adventure for the US government. I walked down the crumbling steps and looked out over the village; crumbling apartment buildings, old houses, a field for playing sports. The place was green, and had a large common pasture. I felt out of place, but welcome. My partner teacher was an effective English teacher, and many students were adept at English. I stepped out and started walking around seeing the sights. Mentally I was exhausted. So much information flooded into my head as I took it all in. I was emotionally open and happy to be here. It smelled of cow plop.

I am trying to recall my first time, stepping out into the sunny day, green and humid. It was a beautiful day, sunlight flickering through the canopied road. I did not know what to feel or think. This was perhaps the clearest moment in my life when I realized I was self-conscious and even timid looking back. I had spent my life in Church or in school. I was on my own. Everyone was watching me constantly. Everyone at your site watches you as you are now the new thing in the village. Villagers have nothing better to do than gossip as they live in a bubble. Despite being in a new environment, spending my life to help enrich others, I felt off about myself. This is the feeling of being in a new place as the proverbial fish out of water. I was on my own and cut off from everything and dumped in the middle of nowhere.

I changed focus to exploring my new environment. I walked over to the courtyard of my school to look around, I sat down on a park bench to take in the world, an old red wooden bench. I thought of the excitement in my new environment, the sun rising on this rustic paradise. I was on my own, cut off from the world in my little mountain kingdom. I didn't even have internet. I started to feel happy here, and I let down my guard. I looked around at the uncut grass, the dirt roads, the green mountains and relaxed in the sun. I sat for a short time taking it all in. I started to get up to explore when I realized something was wrong. I was stuck to the bench. "What the heck?" My first words in my new village on my first day. I put my hand down to push myself off, and I found I was sitting on a freshly painted red bench. After peeling myself off the bench, I walked right back to my home and changed my shorts. The village was still asleep. I stepped back outside, and redid my first attempt. The self-consciousness went right out the window by that point. No one was out yet. There was no wet paint sign, not that that would have changed anything.

I walked around to see the sandy beach on the river where everyone plays. I walked up to the top of the village to the waterfall entrance and found some village ladies setting up their little kiosks for selling tchotchkes to tourists, little knick-knack and honey. I walked up to the restaurant on the waterfall at the base of the mountains. A beautiful little restaurant for outdoor eating by the water, I loved it. I spent my free time here, drinking tea and teaching English. As I left to continue exploring, a woman in a kiosk yelled to me, "Hey American boy, come here." I was horrified. I had been spotted. She was a couple years younger than me and spoke fluent English. I found my first friend.

MARIA'S FAMILY

Maria was a Georgian woman, highly intelligent, spoke three languages, beautiful, and farm girl strong, with broad shoulders. I turned off any inkling of romance. I needed friends, and I followed the golden rule, "never fuck around in your village." She invited me to sit beside her behind the Kiosk. She was selling honey and gave me some as a welcoming gift. This is not like the honey they sell in stores; this was real delicious bee spit. We talked for four hours as we sold honey to tourists. This place was known for the waterfall. I spent the afternoon selling farm products. We played card games while we sat under an old worn umbrella. At one point, her friend came by with an older man. This young woman was eighteen, and the man was clearly in his forties, pot belly, grey hair. I spoke in English assuming she spoke my language, "Oh, is this your father?"

Maria's eyes widened as she turned to me and whispered, "that's her husband."

Thank God her friend did not speak English and neither did her husband. I said in Georgian, "nice to meet you, sassiamovnoa." I said trying to be friendly while Maria was trying to hide her laughter.

She invited me back to her apartment where her family lived. I fell in love with her family. Her grandpa was a tiny old man who fought in the Red Army. He told me stories with the help of Maria. He referred to himself as, "The American's mouse." He was diminutive and in a joking manner, he rested his head on my chest like the scene from *Jurassic Park*, where I was the triceratops, like he wanted to meet an American since he was a kid. They do move in herds. A bizarre moment indeed. I never thought I would find myself in that situation, a Red Army veteran laying his head on my pectoral. Nothing prepared me for that except my humor. He sold vodka in a little stand. I bought vodka from him on occasion, and honey from her on slow days to keep their spirits up.

They invited me for dinner and her whole family came home to see the American standing there. Her father pulled out the homemade vodka and said "Jet Fuel", then set in on fire and handed me a shot. It really did taste like jet fuel. Maria advised me on their culture. It was a humbling moment. I felt like a child learning etiquette. I came to love her family. Maria told her family about the father/husband confusion earlier that day. They all burst out laughing. The father turned to me and said, "Girl is stupid." I spent many nights at her family's place. I usually brought desert; *RC Cola* and ice cream and we made floats in the summer evenings. I really loved that family. Their family lived in those mountains for a thousand years at least. I visited their family cabin which was older than America. It is a shocking timeline for Americans to think about.

Maria's younger brother was mad. We threw brotherly shade at each other in English and Georgian. At one point we yelled insults at each other, then immediately butted heads and threw down in an arm-wrestling contest in an odd macho man moment. His sister called us idiots. We tied in arm wrestling. I was starting to lose when I audibly farted from exertion. Thankfully God granted me a clean fart that evening, which only caused the room to burst into a stalemate of laughter. I had friends and a home.

Maria was not to stay as she was to be married, but we had the summer together as one big family. I met her future husband; she loved him head over heels and she told me he was a goodman. At first when I met him, he was trying to hide his suspicion of me as he saw me as a threat at first. It was a male sexual dominance thing. In their eyes I was tall, exotic American, and "rich". I defused it. I turned to Maria and spoke like an idiot, "Wow, he really handsome." His guard dropped immediately and he laughed. I could read his face, stress diffused and I made a good friend. He liked me. I wished them a happy marriage. From that point on I was the odd American cousin. They invited me to every family event.

On one event, her crazy cousin drove up in his old *Jeep*. We all climbed in to visit her cousins in Batumi. Normally this was a one-hour drive on a small mountain road with occasional guard rails on the cliffs over the river. He gunned the engine and laughed like a lunatic. We made an hour trip in 20 minutes. He popped the vehicle up on two wheels at times, all while flooring it. I think he was sober. It was hard to tell with him. I clicked in the seatbelt and went limp noodle, just in case. Always buckle up in the Peace Corps. I did not see the road or how he drove. I heard it and felt it and figured my best chance of survival was to not care. When a madman is at the wheel, it is best to not know if you are dead or alive. The adrenaline rush made it seem like we teleported. I opened my eyes when they said we arrived. We had a lovely time drinking tea and chatting about marriages.

HOST FAMILY

My government issued family was an average Georgian family. The oldest brother smoked and I constantly told him to quit to their mother's approval. The mother was an intelligent woman who travelled to Turkey for work during the school year. She hated it and missed being with her family. In the summer time she made wonderful meals. She was the heart of the family. I was sad when she left. My host father worked at a parking lot. They were a normal family and I spent time with them whenever I could. I liked them, but the situation became difficult with the food they provided which caused me health problems. It started off with diarrhea, then stomach pain, and it grew worse over time.

They did not have much money. I suspected they signed up for the money. The Peace Corps says the host families sign up because they believe in peace and helping their community. The truth is many families sign up for the money. One volunteer had to change families as her host family hooked a meter up to her bedroom to monitor her electricity use. We received between 200-300 dollars a month to live on, depending on the exchange rate. Half of that went to our host families. I had a friendly family, just not many resources. The father asked for extra money on many occasions. He gambled every weekend. Some volunteers had host families with a large house and ate well. I was not one of them, but there were worse families to live with. In Georgia, almost everyone had to live with a host family.

In the summer, everything was wonderful. I could enjoy life in the Peace Corps and helping others. My host family had a working toilet and a shower so I could bathe and not have to take a bucket bath. I was happy about that. My hair still grew sticky and looked disgusting. This was common amongst everyone as we were told not to bathe every day. I did not spend much time at home in the summer. I went swimming, taught English, exercised, and worked on projects. My first summer there was Peace Corps idyllic.

ALL EYES

The third day there, I spent it in my room reading. I read *Moby Dick* in one day. My mind was overwhelmed due to the completely new environment and stimuli. I had to sit alone the whole day. You need time to process the information. Other volunteers had the same problem at the same time. On the third day everyone needs to mentally rest. Villagers stopped by to check on me while I was trying to sit alone. My host father's sister came into my room while I was reading to spy on me, to see the pet American. Everyone wants to see the American and wants to make friends. All of a sudden, I was popular and trying to keep my privacy in a place that does not value it. Everyone talks about you and you hear rumors about you and everyone spies on you. Its natural in a tiny village, and annoying.

Everyone wondered if I was going to marry a local. I did not, but that did not stop a few women from trying to get close to me. They all wanted to go to the fabled land of wealth. I kept my distance, especially when it was clear the women only wanted a way out of their lives. Some women came up to me and flat out told me they wanted to go to America. Married women with children tried to get close to me. It was disturbing. I was an exotic foreigner everyone confused for being wealthy. I was an average guy from Ohio. If you added in student loans; the locals had more money than I did. It was the illusion of wealth thanks to American media.

My friendly attitude and willingness to help others, teach, and joke made everyone pretty welcoming to me. Although, when I hung my boxers out to dry on the line, everyone commented on my social faux-pas. Apparently, you put all your clothes except the underwear on the drying line. I laughed and pointed out my boxers were the American flag, and should hang in the breeze as any normal flag. I had purchased them especially for the Peace Corps. The locals laughed at the stupidity of it. I thought it was hysterical and threw a salute to my boxers. They flew in the breeze, old stars and stripes between my knees.

THE AMERICAN TAX

I did not think it was funny when someone stole the insoles of my running shoes. My host mother had moved my shoes to the shoe rack in the hallway outside the apartment with everyone else's shoes. Someone stole only the insoles of both shoes, and left the shoes. I asked her what happened and she said dogs probably grabbed them. Right, like dogs came up to steal both insoles and left the shoes without teeth marks. That was the only thing anyone ever stole from me in the Peace Corps. I did not give a second chance. If you talked to the locals about it, they will say it was an animal and that no one in their village is a thief. They will cover for each other. I came to help these people, and they stole from me in my first month. Do not expect anything different. To the people you help, you are just money and they will steal anything they can from you.

Locals tried to charge me double at every opportunity they could, at restaurants, on a bus, in stores. They will try to cheat you any way possible. I had to shock them by speaking Georgian, "hey I live here." This is the best way to stop a con artist. I call it the American Tax, and they will get you anyway they can, food, clothes, anything. Prepare to pay an extra 30% on everything. I came here to help them and they felt happy to rip me off. Noble intentions and sacrifice do not matter, all they do is cheat you. Volunteers are just wealthy tourists. My belief in humanity went out the door in the Peace Corps.

I went to restaurants and stores with Maria and other friends and they introduced me to honest merchants. They still ripped me off, just not as bad. That is how you know who your friend is. You have to have a Georgian connection. That is key to seeing the beauty of Georgian hospitality. Georgians keep each other in line.

You have to be careful when your pay is pennies and you depend on others for food. If you were not a wealthy American like me, you had to live on the tiny stipend. The wealthiest volunteer of my group spent the equivalent of a monthly stipend on a Saturday night in Tbilisi. He spent in one hour what I made in a month, on partying and drinking. Volunteers are not "supposed" to as it is against the "should" rules, but the Peace Corps only acts when their image is under attack. The Peace Corps looks the other way as long as they do not get a complaint. You can spend your own money, as it makes the American government look better. For some volunteers, the Peace Corps is one big tax payer paid vacation.

MORNING WORKOUT AND LANGUAGE LESSONS

I launched several small month-long projects to figure out the English level of the students in the village. I did this voluntarily and wanted to learn more about the education in the village. I tutored for a month of free lessons to six different groups. This allowed me to plan future projects off of a few sample groups. Even the Country Director made fun of me for working in the summer.

I launched a morning workout team. Twice a week I led a group of college and high school students for morning exercise. We jogged for four kilometers full trip, a short distance to stay healthy and active. One guy was annoying and wanted to prove how strong he was compared to the American. There is always one. He pointed out how slow I was at jogging as he jogged faster than me; he did not have a surgically repaired knee. After our jog, we went to the beach near the river for pushups and swimming. He started taunting me during pushups, "You American, you are big, but not strong, you are weak." I ignored him until he started poking me in the chest right after I got up from pushups. He screeched as I grabbed him, picked him up, and body slammed him into the sand. I sat on him until he gave up. I stood up, then helped him up, "Ok, you are strong." We were friends after that.

I asked if anyone else wanted to try. The body builder nihilist sailor shook his head, "We're not all idiots." I liked him, he was funny and chiseled like a Greek god. His mother hated the fact he was a nihilist. We got along great. We continued to work out in the mornings and enjoyed the summer life. After our workouts we swam in the river to clean up a bit. Some of the young men invited me to visit a brothel with them. They were proud that they knew Russian prostitutes. It was a good level of cultural acceptance, but I declined the offer for a few thousand microbial reasons.

FORUM ON THE BEACH

Bring a towel. Most of the village spent the summer on the beach of the river sunbathing, fishing, and swimming. After my workout, I ate and rested, worked on projects and lesson planned. In the afternoon I went to the beach. I'd walk down the rocks to the sandy beach and find my friends/ host brothers/students and relax with them. All the fathers were there and they drank on the beach with their sons and relaxed. I joined in and spent part of my stipend on buying beer and peanuts. Other times I bought ice cream for my students if I saw them near the shop or if they were hanging out with me. I made sure to contribute.

Some of the older generations complained about America to me, things they heard, and stated that Georgia was a far superior country and community. I did not argue with them but tried to give a fair and balanced explanation. When it came to the power structures of America and Georgia, I could not see any difference. Both countries have a small group of rich people at the top controlling everything, with everyone else broke at the bottom. Same crap, different country. They agreed when I told them their lives were better here by the river than stuck in a cubicle in Ohio. The less I argued with them, and the more I agreed, the more they bought me beer. The more I explained both the good and bad about America, the more they listened to me. I was not going to argue over which country was best, the answer was obvious, Canada. NO ONE DISAGREED WITH ME.

Only an idiot argues over useless political opinions. I listened and added in info from myside to give a more realistic view. The subject that horrified them the most was the American healthcare system. They were horrified to hear lifesaving medicine that was free for them, costed hundreds of dollars in America. As I explained costs in America, the pro-Americans were slack-jawed, the Georgian nationalists laughed. "Yeah, Americans have died because they can't afford insulin." Then they called me a spy. That is when the argument started. I defended myself by asking the two greatest questions, "How many people are in your village? How many cows? Is this number equal? Then if I am a spy, I would have had to sleep with my boss's wife to get sent to this village." They laughed at the logic behind it. Most of the time we talked about movies.

I went for a swim in between rounds of the beach debates. That river was fast, but slowly over time I grew stronger and stronger. I reached the height of my physical strength here. I exercised four hours every day. Swimming upstream was a great way to strength train. Had to be careful though, people drowned here every few years. For the most part, I spent every day making friends, swimming, working out, writing, teaching English, and project planning. I did more work than what was required by the Peace Corps. I wanted to show my support to the community. Everyone wanted to take me to their house for dinner.

RESTAURANT OF MEMORIES

After my time at the beach, I spent the evenings at the restaurant, drinking tea, writing, thinking, joking, tutoring students. I was happy here. The hot summer air, the cool river. I would only show up in off hours so as not to interfere with business. The village elder and owner appreciated it. The food they served was phenomenal. Meat grilled to perfection, chunks of pork, beef, mutton, grilled slowly over glowing embers, and the spices... I tasted the ash on my lips. In the summer I ate there every Friday night, bought barbecue, enjoyed a nice meal and watched the sun set over the mountains. At closing time, I helped clean up, busted tables, swept, translated for tourists, updated the menu in English, and tutored. Many of my high school students worked there and they sat and talked with me when it was slow. They were happy to have a free tutoring lesson. The parents were equally happy to have me there. The owners' grandchildren received free tutoring so they plied me with all the free tea I could drink, a deal I jumped on. My tea addiction came from here.

Many of my students sat with me in the evenings talking, drinking tea with me. On young man asked me about America, I told him the reality of it. I showed him music from around the world; I got him to fall in love with *The Kinks*. His father was hard on him, I could read it on his face. We played backgammon together. I taught him tactics as best I could.

The restaurant owner's brother and my student's great uncle found me fascinating and challenged me to a backgammon tournament. I beat him three times in a row. His brother mocked him, "What, the American too good for you?" I never lost a game while I was there. I studied backgammon extensively that summer. I sat with my students' fathers over backgammon and khachapuri and talked history. It was shocking to hear the stories of Stalin's purges, here were the living stories. It was an eye opener.

This restaurant had so many positive memories for me. One rainy afternoon without any tourists around, a college student brought out a hookah. She lit the charcoal cube, inhaled, and handed it to me. I did a double check to make sure it was not anything illegal, to the laughter of everyone around. The village elder asked me if I wanted something else. I declined the offer. My students, their older siblings, and I sat there passing the hookah around on a rainy day under the awning, blowing smoke into the rain. Raindrops slashed through the flavored clouds. It was watermelon tobacco in the mountain rain that really altered my state of mind, to really embrace life after Ohio. I fell in love with the people and my community, as a crazy American cousin. That's what kept me going despite it all. I can still remember the red pipe, inhaling and puffing away and joking in broken Georgian and broken English. There is something clean about hookah smoke, it reminded me of incense. One of those holy moments from an apathetic universe. I told everyone to stay away from cigarettes.

Other nights I sat with lady police cadets who liked to flirt with me. They took me with them to steal corn from a local farm. We walked along the road at night and dived into the corn field when a car drove by. One lady cadet started plucking corn and threw ear after ear to me. I only learned it was stolen after it was eaten. We carried our husked loot back to the restaurant where we grilled it up. It was a black evening. Smoke poured into the night sky from the charcoal. Food is so much tastier when you steal it with cops. The lady cop devoured the burnt kernels as I joined in. Corn stuck to our teeth, sweat dripped from humidity, slapping mosquitos.

Other evenings I sat and chatted with the ladies who ran the kitchen. I joked with them when work was over and I helped clean up. My nihilistic sailor friend liked working shirtless at the restaurant. One day, he jumped up and flexed at his lifelong friend who was eyeing him, she blushed at his bronze six pack. He is the peak of human beauty; I am not. I jumped up and ripped off my shirt in the same motion and the same enthusiasm. With my pale skin, I stuck out my gut and struck the same pose. Everyone burst out laughing at the sheer failure. The sailor's female friend said between laughs, "Never do that again." I got the laugh, I won.

I decided to be more courageous at this time. The volunteer from the town over came to the restaurant with his colleagues. They invited me along as I helped them with projects. I helped everyone I could. After dinner we were joking and getting ready to leave. They had some leftover jet fuel vodka. I poured myself a shot, borrowed a lighter, and blew a fireball over the table. The fire only went out about three feet, but it was bright orange. They all applauded me, asking if I had ever done that before. "Thank you, thank you, first time." Fun little party trick. Who else could claim they learned how to breathe fire in the Peace Corps? Breathing fire is not against the rules in the Peace Corps.

AKSANA

I grew close with one of the waitresses at the restaurant. She spoke four languages and loved to joke with me. She was out of college. She came from a poor family who lived four to a two-room shanty. Many families lived like this, with no money, cramped into a small apartment, sharing beds, but oddly enough they had a community. Communities are built on reliance and need for others, as well as a common background. The wealthier families could afford a bed for every kid. This family did not have a hundred dollars between them. I hung out and joked with Aksana and everyone gossiped we would get married. We drank tea and studied together at the restaurant. I studied Georgian, she studied Turkish. She took me to her favorite church and we prayed together, as she was deeply religious. We walked by the river and tossed coins into it and made a wish together. She never told me what her wish was, but it was important to her.

One morning she joined me for a jog. After the jog, we went down to the river. She told me no one had ever taught her to swim. She dived into the water with all her clothes on. I dived in too. I taught her the basics in the shallows and shew quickly learned. By the time she left the river she knew how to swim. No one bothered to teach her yet she lived by a river her whole life. That afternoon we drank coffee and watched an old Bollywood disco film together. Everyone assumed we would get married, but it never happened. We could be seen every week drinking tea and studying together. She was my friend. She eventually married a Georgian man and moved away. I was so happy for them both.

SUMMER EDUCATION CAMP

The Peace Corps has every teacher volunteer organize a summer camp for the kids during their first summer. I met all the teachers and we planned a week-long event. I enlisted the aid of Ms. Lisa once again. She was the greatest teacher I ever met, one who often said, "Don't expect school to educate you." We led classroom projects, did scavenger hunts, watched a movie in English, and all the summer school fun kids could want. Everything went as you would expect from a summer English camp. On the last day we had a water balloon toss for all the kids. I had saved one balloon and hurled it at Ms. Lisa. She moved faster than I had thought possible. She was gracefully quick on her feet and moved like a dancer, at least when a water balloon was hurled at her. We reported the project as a success.

Ms. Lisa and I sat together in the hot evenings and watched the sun set over the mountains while we soaked in the river. As much as we loved the places we were at, it was stressful. We were being watched by everyone. The hardest part was what Lisa said, she revealed what had been stressing her. By this point, only four or five months in, I was still naïve about many things.

"This isn't what I signed up for. They said helping people who need help. These people have everything, why are we here? They have money. I mean look around, this place is well above the development index, and we're out here helping a country who doesn't need it. There's no reason for us to be here. Do you think America would accept help like this from another country?"

"Hey, I'm just following orders", I said.

Her next words hit home like a hammer fall, "Like a good little Nazi."

It hit like a hurricane, but I laughed at it. It was the Nazi defense. Here I was supposedly helping the world, defending myself like a Nazi. I was in the face of superior logic. I relented, "They wouldn't allow anything, we're too proud and told too much we are the greatest."

"These people have everything." She was frustrated.

I could not help but agree, "Many of these families have more money than me. I'm poorer than the people I came to help. Maybe not Aksana, but she's the poorest girl in the village."

Lisa went over a lot of things America has done in the past. I gave up the moral high ground and faced reality in the river that night. I said as much to her. "While we're here, we might as well help out the kids as much as possible. Give them a good fighting chance and tell them not to flee their country for ours. Show them reality."

Lisa nodded. "I like you; you have a code you follow." I took that as a mark of honor from her. I never thought about it before, but I was raised with high moral standards in a devout Catholic family.

"I thought I came here to help people; they don't need help. Where do we go from here?"

"Anywhere that will accept your help, you're a good writer." She had seen some of my work in training. She thought it was good. It was a first draft of a never completed story.

"I ain't that good, but thanks. All support is welcome."

Every night we talked history. Every night I learned something about America's foreign relations and how the Peace Corps fits into it. I left the river every night a haunted man. I was still a patriot, but I was now questioning it. We dried off on the beach. "You ever need help, call me. I'll be there in a day."

We sat late into the night at the restaurant eating barbecue, joking about history and the 90's. I had literature, she had history. We compared notes and filled in the blanks for each other. While chatting, massive bullfrogs hopped out of the shadows all around us. Some as big as my head. A cat came over and started batting at one. The bullfrog turned and backhanded the cat. We were perturbed by the toad. "Are those thumbs?" Those huge bullfrogs had massive forearms. We decided not to bother the toads when one hopped on the table and starred at us. The bullfrog was huge.

We spent our last day together in Batumi. We found a hostel and dropped off our bags and headed for the beach. We sunbathed and swam in cycles. Late in the afternoon, we grabbed a bite to eat from a small restaurant and then headed to the tallest hotel in the city. We sat in a bar on the top floor and bought ourselves a couple of black beers and watched the sunset over the Black Sea. We relaxed in the clouds and watched the sunset over the endless watery horizon. The next morning, I helped Lisa find a taxi for the next part of her journey. I waved goodbye as she flicked me off from the window of the car. I returned the salute. I was alone again. I was never the same ideologically. I began to question everything. The most important thing in American culture is the image you want to project. I would learn that lesson from the Peace Corps soon enough.

COUNTRY DIRECTOR'S VISIT

He came out once to visit Peace Corps Volunteers in their villages. He had a personal driver and a big government SUV, all paid for by the US government. I do not believe he ever stepped into a normal marshrutka crammed with thirty people. He came in, promised everyone peanut butter then went around seeing all the tourist sights. I noticed something unusual about him. He had his wrist watch on upside down, with the face of the watch under his palm, military style. I only knew this because a veteran told me about it. He told us he worked with military intelligence in Afghanistan in the foreign service right before he worked in the Peace Corps. This should tell you the level of military influence throughout the US government. Nothing is distant from the US military, and the Peace Corps is no different. What was he doing here? When no one was in listening distance, I suggested, "sir, you might want to turn your watch right side up."

He smiled a knowing smile through broad teeth, "it's just upside down," he emphasized the words confidently. He was still thinking like them. Whenever I spoke with him, I felt odd, like he was two people in one. Like one was nice, and there was something else hidden. After he saw the waterfall and some of the tourist sites, he walked by the kiosks of the old women. He stopped to buy from a few different sellers. He told me, "I bought something from everyone to keep your name safe. Buy from everyone."

"Thank you, sir, I did that my first week."

"Of course, you did, because you're a diplomat." He said sarcastically. Standard foreign service mentality, buy your friends. I had been buying from all different stores at different intervals to make sure I supported the growth of the community. I even did my best to buy only Georgian products.

The only other thing he did on his visit was tell the volunteers, "I never get tired of being thanked for all your hard work." He never thanked us, but stated he liked how others thanked him for our work. Then he droned on praising himself. "I used you volunteers as an excuse to get more funding. When I request additional funds, I always say it's for the welfare of the volunteers. That way, no one can argue. You have to have the right excuse for everything." To sum up the conversation, he loved getting praised for the work of others, and then told us how to lie. The Peace Corps will teach you how to lie and make excuses like a trained diplomat.

We received no additional funding in our stipend. We were paid about 200-300 dollars a month, and we were not paid in dollars, but in Lari. It was around 750 Lari every month, and it never changed, no matter the value of the currency. Peace Corps Georgia receives the funds for volunteers from the government in dollars. Due to fluctuations in the exchange rate, if we had been paid in dollars, we would have had more money in concerns to the local economy. Peace Corps Georgia kept the difference from the exchange rate for their own funding. The US government sends the funds in dollars, and the budget is fixed in dollars, the Peace Corps exchanges it, and gives the volunteers a fixed stipend in Lari, the local currency. The Peace Corps keeps any excess Lari from the exchange, and the value of the Lari fluctuates in a predictable manner. In winter, when the program converts the currency, Peace Corps Georgia has a budget increase of about of 20-30% due to the exchange. Volunteers in Georgia had less spending power than the volunteers of other countries who were paid in dollars. Does this mean the volunteers get more money depending on the season? No, volunteers are paid the same amount in

Lari, no matter what. The extra money from the conversion goes into the operations budget for whatever use the director deemed suitable. For our Country Director, that meant challenge coins and a Thanksgiving dinner where the hotel charged the Peace Corps with an excessive bill citing damages. I later found a small jar of peanut butter in my mail box at the HQ with a note in the Country Director's handwriting, saying, "as promised." It was a bribe.

"It's for the welfare of the volunteers" is what Peace Corps employees say when they want more funding. Yet when a volunteer asks for funding to meet the basic requirements to live, they are told, "You must respect the taxpayer dollar", by the same people. No one in the US government cares about the tax payer. The Peace Corps does not care about the volunteers.

BACK BREAKING VOLUNTEER

After a summer of working on projects and helping other volunteers, school came around. The last weekend of the summer I spent the evening hanging out at the restaurant drinking tea and speaking in English. As I was leaving the restaurant, I walked down a set of narrow concrete steps and slipped. I tried to catch myself, but I landed hard on my back. I was sprawled out and in shock. When I realized I could move, I was in severe pain. I slowly got up and limped home to bed and tried to sleep it off. The next morning, I woke up in worse pain. I called the doctors and they sent me to the hospital in Batumi.

I was scared and in severe pain. The neighbor drove me, and when I got to the hospital, the medical personnel placed me on a gurney and rushed me into a hallway and had me wait. I could barely walk or move as each step sent shock waves. I lay there alone on a gurney for a long time, starring up at the ceiling. I wondered if this was the end of my Peace Corps service, if I would be permanently injured, or a thousand other worries ran through my head. Spinal injuries are no laughing matter. I lay there feeling nothing but pain every time I breathed. I tried to be as still as possible. I had trouble focusing in Georgian. I lay there for probably a half hour before the doctor came out.

If I thought I was worried before, when the doctor came out, it was amplified a thousand times. He looked like a KGB henchman from the movies. He was massive, shaved head, broad features, gold chain, large hands ending in surprisingly well manicured finger nails. An odd observation from a gurney, but I always pay attention to a doctor's hands. His face had all the expressiveness of a cement statue. I will remember his words for the rest of my life, "Today we break you."

My eyes widened, and I went still. He paused seeing my reaction. "No, no... um today you broke?" I was never so relieved to hear broken English in my life. I breathed out a little laugh. I said what happened in broken Georgian, at the same time showing with my hands what happened. A nurse translated the story for him. He lifted up my legs slowly with his huge hands. I yelped in pain. He said something to a nurse in Georgian, "...MRI." He gave me a thumbs up as they wheeled me away. Most confident thumbs up I ever saw. The man could have broken concrete with those thumbs.

They wheeled me to the MRI. I sat there for an hour in the machine as I tried to remain still with every breathe causing me pain. A thousand thoughts running through my head, being sent back, needing surgery, all my hard work ruined by slipping on steps. I sat in that tube an hour, hearing the loud buzz of the machinery. Then I was moved to the waiting room for two hours, where I lay perfectly still. The doctor came back with a translator, "You have contusion – and sprain along the spine and on your hips and ankle. You can walk, but need crutches and two weeks rest and therapy. The bone is bruised, not broken. Impact was not on the spine." I was so happy to yelp in pain. The doctor laughed when I told him I loved him in Russian. He had the most childlike smile I had ever seen compared to a face that looked like it screamed *Kalashnikov*. My host family took me home.

The Peace Corps doctor asked me on the phone, "How did you manage to hit to the right of the spine? That fall should have paralyzed you; it was off by three centimeters from dead center." I love when a doctor tells me I should have been paralyzed.

"I know to never fall straight back, so I rolled slightly. I tried catching myself with my ankle and sprained it instead of landing on my spine."

She laughed, "If you hit your head at that fall, it could have killed you. How did you miss your head?"

"I tucked my head forward." When I fell, I tried to catch myself and ended up bruising my elbow and spraining my ankle and my back. It was enough to divert the main impact away from the spine. She laughed and told me to stay in bed for two weeks and then told me to do physical therapy on myself as they could not help me. She told me to look up some exercises online. The doctors told me to take care of my problem myself. The Peace Corps' answer to my medical problem was to give me a cane for my limp and to browse the internet for a solution.

"Had you been drunk; you would have been fine. Next time drink," she said. I had a back injury and the doctor told me I should have been drinking.

This was how I missed the first two weeks of class, in bed, in pain, alone. This was a miserable time. I could barely walk and could not leave the apartment. I was in pain without any internet, and no way to contact people outside of my Peace Corps phone. I sat and watched two movies over and over for the two weeks. It felt like my back was broken in several places. Every time I moved, it felt like my body was cracking apart. My hips felt like broken glass. The injury covered me entire back. My back felt like how a shattered dinner plate looks. I was alone for these two weeks as everyone went about their day. I read everything I could and fixed my clothes and tried to stay busy. I grew depressed. Two weeks of sitting alone with nothing to do in a foreign country is miserable. I wrote, but I was isolated. My mental health took a beating as much as my back. I tried to do what I could, but isolation is isolation. I had to carry on for my belief in helping others and serving my country, which was my priority. Eventually I could walk on my own without a cane. I still had backpain and numbness on the sites of impact, and I was stiff as a board. The price I paid to serve America. I had to walk slowly, but I started teaching after two weeks.

This injury, the back pain, the ankle pain, and the numbness plagued me the rest of my service. The broken infrastructure and mountain environment proved to be a nightmare for trying to heal a severely sprained ankle and back. It seemed like every week I twisted my ankle on a broken walkway or on ice. I did stretches and what I could, but my body never fully healed. I needed physical therapy. The Peace Corps doctors would not send me back to America for physical therapy, and they would not send me anywhere in Georgia for treatment either. They did not advise me on anything either, or even bother to show me exercises. They told me there was nothing they could do. I complained and reported it to the Peace Corps doctors multiple times, and they told me to fix it myself. They did nothing to fix the problem.

They did do something. The Peace Corps sent me to get an X-ray for soft tissue damage. Then they told me I was fine and sent me back to my village. I was still in pain and still limping. This was when I learned the truth of the Peace Corps; the Peace Corps has no real interest in keeping their volunteers healthy. The Peace Corps is only interested in doing the bare minimum to avoid any legal responsibility. If anything, the Peace Corps only treats the symptom and never cares about fixing the cause. Why, because the Peace Corps has the volunteer for two years, and it is cheaper to get rid of the volunteer and get a new one.

It took a year after my medical termination from the Peace Corps for my ankle heal, two years from the injury. Even to today, there is still numbness on the spot where I hit my back. The Peace Corps lied to me. When I volunteered, they said all my medical problems would be taken care of. The US government denied medical care for my injury after I was medically terminated by the Peace Corps for my injuries. I had to pay for my own physical therapist for months to get the injury healed as much as possible. Then the physical therapist discovered I had sustained nerve damage to my back. To this day, I have numbness near my spine, three centimeters from center, at the site of impact. The Peace Corps told me to fix the problem myself, and then refused medical care from an injury I received while serving. The welfare of volunteers is not a priority for the Peace Corps, but a responsibility to avoid. The Peace Corps only treats symptoms.

THAT'S MR. TEACHER

Being absent for the first two weeks of school, I had to play catch-up. On my first day, my partner teacher's cousin died. I volunteered to teach our classes alone so she could tend to her family. The Peace Corps says that volunteers will not teach on their own, but they still do. Even better, the other English teacher heard I was working on my own and left without telling me. She ditched me on my first day. She didn't even know any English, so why was she teaching? This is a frustrating reality within the Peace Corps. I did a crash course on names and introductions, using the more advanced English speakers to help others. By the end of the day, my back was killing me and I wanted to jump into the river and float away.

The majority of the kids were wonderful, willing to learn and listen. I did my best to be as encouraging and supportive as possible. I loved seeing the kids smile at stupid English jokes or when I read a story. That made my partner teacher fall in love with me. She said I would make a great father one day, then she tried to set me up with a relative. At one point, I noticed a child struggling with her right hand while coloring. There was no physical disability that I could see. I asked the child which hand was easier to color with, putting up my hands in front of me while I kneeled beside her, she picked my left hand. She was a south-paw, and trying to use her right hand. I encouraged her to use her left and suddenly school was easier for her. I did not want her developing a stutter. The third-graders often tried to get me to say "butt," while the twelfth-graders wanted me to say "cock". Not much changes except the vocabulary. All grades wanted me to read to them. If the students behaved, I would read a story at the end of class. This was something they all agreed with. They loved learning and loved the stories far more than anything else.

The best linguist I ever met on the face of the earth was my second-grade student. She loved learning and her mind was like a sponge. I spoke and she flawlessly mimicked all of my words to the letter, correct pronunciation, perfect syntax, it was startling. In one hour, she copied everything I said and used it to make her own sentences, even matching my accent. This second grader was the smartest person I ever met. She was a genius through and through. Her name was Catherine the Awesome.

Catherine had a sister in the fourth grade, she was just as smart, but gosh darn, she was devious. Catherine's older sister learned that her smile could get her out of trouble. The bigger her smile the worse the offense. She was the troublemaker in class, but she did it sparingly. I learned this when she snuck into the teacher's desk and stole a bag of chocolates and shared them with her friends before class. I discovered her devious side when I walked into the classroom one morning and she had a huge smile. I was suspicious. I examined the classroom; all the kids were eerily quiet. I held my hand out in front of her and told her to give me whatever it was. Right in front of me she passed the candy under the desk to her friend. I saw it through a small gap in the row of desks. "I am not blind, and that was your last chance for reading today." All of a sudden, the kids handed over the chocolates choosing the reading over the sweets. They were smart kids. She was devious. The only challenge I had in class was a child that had ADHD. He was constantly... "oh hey, a butterfly." I had to find ways of keeping him engaged, usually fun activities and stories kept him centered. The boring tedious grammar lessons did not work at all.

I discovered pronunciation problems and had to think on my feet to get the children to overcome them. The word "the", the lynchpin of English, was causing trouble for the kids in my class. All the kids were saying "teh". I shook my head, pronouncing "th" clearer. They tried, but they did not want to stick their tongues out as it was inappropriate in their culture. English is all spoken with the front of the mouth, while Georgian was spoken in the back. I switched to absurdity to be logical. I slapped the back of my head and launched my tongue out of my mouth in a ridiculous way, then pronounced "the" with my tongue sticking out. The kids started laughing, and then stuck their tongues out and finally pronounced it correctly. I pulled on my ear lobe to act as a retracting switch for my tongue, which made the kids laugh even more. My partner teacher said, "you will make a great father one day." I thanked her for the kind reply.

I had to crack down on cheating in class. Kids were passing notes back and forth and cheating on tests. I ended up tearing up several tests in front of them when they were caught. The students were shocked. They started realizing that cheating did not fly with me. Only after realizing there was nothing to gain, they relented.

For the seventh-graders, I had to be creative with projects and classwork. My goal was to get them to think outside of the box, and work on creative problem solving. One of my favorite class games was to write numbers or words on the chalkboard and they would hit the correct number with a fly swatter, like that game every kid in America played for Spanish class. I changed the game halfway through, and said "desk", something that was not on the board. The goal was to get them to realize the rules had changed and now they had to operate without visible cues. I did this with the advanced students first. I said desk. The students looked around and were confused, "It's not on the board teacher."

"I know what is on the board, desk."

They looked at me confused, then thought for a second. The smartest girl in the class figured it out and cautiously hit the desk with the swatter. I smiled, "Correct." It worked. I changed the rules for different games and tasks, and forced them to think and adapt. It proved to be useful. Teachers from other schools were interested in this method, and the super intendent of the region made a note of it. I always tried to have the students think on their feet.

I had the high schoolers bring in their favorite songs. I broke the lyrics down and taught via their interests. They loved it, as now they could contribute to the lesson. I had to cancel a few songs as some of the smarter students started bringing in songs with clearly inappropriate vocabulary. One student was mortified when I explained the lyrics to *Creep* by *Radiohead*, she thought it was a love song. The only real troublemaker was a guy who liked to set the trashcan on fire.

Georgia has a severe equality problem, where the women of their culture are second class-citizens and live as domestic slaves. This translated to the classroom. I had trouble motivating the boys to stop smoking and start learning. I had to break down the cost of smoking and show them how much money they were wasting. To get the boys motivated to learn English, I had to use a tried-and-true method. The boys in class did not want to learn English and were apathetic to learning in general. They all said Georgian is good enough. I turned and asked all the young ladies in class, "Who wants a husband in the future?" All raised their hands. "Who wants a husband who only speaks Georgian?" No hands went up. The boys looked nervous in their chairs. They listened after that.

I launched several after school programs focused on English conversation and freestyle teaching. It was designed to be a no stress environment, free of grades. A lot of these kids wanted to learn English and improve their lives, only their ability to grow and learn was limited. I have many good memories of teaching and helping kids learn. I was dedicated to helping those kids anyway I could. I loved being a volunteer. Even with my constant health problems, I never gave up. If I saw my students on a bus when going to the next town over, I made funny faces at them to make them laugh. Adults would look back at me, and I acted nonchalant like nothing happened. They all knew I was the American teacher. If the students caught me in the shop, I bought them sunflower seeds or ice cream; even for the twelfth-grade boys who hated school.

There was one disturbing moment in class that I remember being told about, and every volunteer needs to be prepared for. A ninth-grade boy hit a girl in class. The only thing the school could do was yell at him. He did it when I was absent, and when my partner teacher was out of the room. This tells you how prevalent violence against women is in Georgia. I can only assume where he learned that behavior. The biggest problem in Georgia is how women are treated, and it goes far beyond classroom behavior.

HOME SWEET GULAG, MIND THE HUMOR

As soon as the school year started, my host mother left for work and I would not see her until the next year. Once she left, everything grew worse at home. The family was to provide two meals for me a day as per Peace Corps requirements. In the summer, she made all sorts of wonderful dishes. Once she left, it was nothing but potatoes. The father skipped buying much of anything else. We ate nothing but potatoes and bread. It was like this for the next six months. Day in, day out, potato. Maybe once every couple of weeks we had beans, and I was thankful for that. I was so happy when bean day came around, I laughed and smiled, and was happy again. I grew weak on that diet, and lost a lot of weight. I started to have health problems; my stomach hurt every day and I had diarrhea after every meal. The food made me sick, nothing but greasy fried potatoes. I had no energy, and I felt exhausted all the time. The only thing that kept me going was my drive to serve America, helping my community, and the vitamin tablets the doctor gave me.

There was nothing but potato. Potato. I began to hate potatoes, breakfast, dinner, potato. Potato. He was given enough money to buy different foods, but he bought a big bag of potatoes and that was it. When it came to food, I have never met anyone cheaper than him. It caused me so many health problems. I had to have multiple surgeries because of this, it devastated my body. Let me put it this way: I was in my mid-twenties and I was down to my weight from middle school. It was difficult living with this family. I had to look at it this way. He came from a poor family. Was he friendly? Yes, he was. Was he cheap? Definitely. Did this cause me to have a bunch of health problems? Yes, it did. Did he gamble every weekend? Yes, he did. Did he sign up for the money? That is a given. On multiple occasions he asked me for additional money, which he was told not to do. I paid him everything the Peace Corps told me, and nothing more. That is a line a volunteer can never cross. On the other hand, if I ever received a care package, I shared what I had with the host family and my students.

My host father never believed me when I said how much money I made in the Peace Corps. I was paid in Lari, and he was confused and thought I had a large salary. I was income to him. This is common in the Peace Corps; host families will sign up for the money and treat it like income. I heard similar stories from other volunteers, and this is true across the globe. It is more common than the Peace Corps will admit. This is the stupid part, the Peace Corps tells their volunteers the families sign up because they believe in the mission, and they specifically say that no family does it for the money. Another Peace Corps bureaucratic lie, they are not going to tell the truth because that would invite questions. I missed living with the Soviet police. Volunteers are forced to live with a host family in Georgia, unless the volunteer can find another place to live under a tiny budget. Most of the time, there are no other places to rent in Georgia. There was no choice in my village.

You cannot afford to live on a Peace Corps stipend independently in Georgia, but of course the Peace Corps says you can. Every volunteer I met who lived independently in Georgia was using their own money from America. Here is the problem. Georgia has a higher standard of living than many Peace Corps countries. Georgia was never a third world country by any means. It is part of Eastern Europe, an EU candidate, and the former USSR, which means a higher cost and standard of living. The cheapest apartment I ever heard of in Georgia, while I served, was three hundred dollars, and they wanted the rent in dollars, not Lari. This was far more than our monthly stipend, which is supposed to include the costs of food and rent.

The Peace Corps is not going to spend more on volunteers, because that would break the illusion of why they claim they are in Georgia. I have seen pictures from volunteers from African Peace Corps programs who could afford spacious apartments on their stipend. This is not the case in Georgia. The problem comes from the fact that the Peace Corps is forcing a stipend that works well for Third World countries, onto a Second World post-soviet country. The Peace Corps adjusts their stipend for each country, but the difference is not that much from country to country. Georgia has never been classified as a Third World country, because it is technically a Second World country due to being part of the former Soviet Union. Georgia was nowhere close to being as underdeveloped as a colonized African country. The Peace Corps says it is in Georgia to help develop the country after Soviet colonization. This is partially true as Georgia was controlled by the Soviet Union and does need help, but it was nowhere as bad as what Europe did to Africa. The Georgian SSR was also one of the wealthiest countries in the Soviet Union in concerns to material wealth. The Peace Corps never mentioned that.

The real reason the Peace Corps is in Georgia is to prevent the return of the Soviet Union, contain Russian influence, and to spread NATO. This can be verified by the entrance of the Peace Corps programs into Eastern Europe in the 90's, and those countries subsequently joining NATO. Those Eastern European countries were developed enough, they just needed to be Americanized to facilitate the transition to NATO. The Peace Corps was sent in to convert the people to western ideology, and that is the purpose of the Peace Corps.

The Soviet Union was nowhere close to being as underdeveloped as Africa, but the Peace Corps still has to fit the image and the budget of a Peace Corps program onto a European country. To save money, they force the volunteers to live with host families as it is cheaper to rent a room than an apartment. The Peace Corps would have to double or even triple the stipend of a Peace Corps Volunteer in Georgia to allow a volunteer to be able to even afford a small apartment. The Peace Corp does not care about the welfare of the volunteer, as long as they don't die. The Peace Corps calculates the stipend on the sole determination of renting a room, which brings the cost down to comparable levels of other Peace Corps programs. Every country is different, but in Georgia, volunteers only get a room. Volunteers are expected to live under the host family's expectations, which every volunteer is frustrated with and there are many problems stemming from this. One volunteer tried studying the language with screaming children running around every night and had to move. For myself, my health deteriorated due to the family diet. There are many more stories. The Peace Corps goes out of their way to emphasize volunteers are free to be themselves in their own room. Living independently is a luxury Peace Corps Georgia. All volunteers I met who lived on their own were paying out of pocket.

I lost weight rapidly. I started spending the rest of my stipend on buying food at a nearby shop to keep my calories up. I had to go into Batumi every other week to buy a salad and eat vegetables. I downed vitamins like candy, but my health took a beating. My host father's cooking involved massive amounts of oil. Think of a bowl of oil, now add a potato, that was the food. I had diarrhea every day. I began having digestive track issues which plagued me for the rest of my tour on top of everything else, culminating in me needing multiple surgeries. I developed polyps and parts of my stomach were eroded away. The pain in my stomach was growing so bad it caused me to wear a hole through my sweaters as I was constantly rubbing my stomach to settle the pain. I woke up in the middle of the night with stomach cramps many times. It was like this the rest of my time in the Peace Corps, and I did report my problems, nothing was done to correct them. I had so many medical problems, yet I carried on, believing in the Peace Corps. The Peace Corps did nothing.

When winter crept around, everything became freezing cold. Our only heat was a small wood burning stove. It heated the main room, but my room was frozen. I froze every single night. I was lucky to find a spare sleeping bag on the free table. I went to bed wearing two pairs of socks, two pairs of pajamas, a long shirt, a hoodie, and I was still cold. To sleep, I climbed into a sleeping bag under four or five blankets. It was bitter cold. I stopped shaving just to stay warm. I woke up every morning with frost in my beard. I became very thin, but I still got up, forced myself to smile, did my pushups and stretched. When I moved, it sounded like a glacier breaking apart. I came to serve America and world peace and ended up in a Gulag. It took a toll on me, all the isolation, the cold, the diet, and the health problems. My insides hurt, my back, my leg. I got out of bed feeling broken, went to bed feeling broken. Every time I crawled out of my greasy cocoon, I heard every single joint crack.

I worked like a dog, helping everyone I could, and yet I felt empty. I felt to no real joy, or anything. I was being pushed to the end of my limits and being ground down in these conditions. There was no happiness, it was unpaid work, endless grammar, tests, potatoes, freezing winter and pain. Who could be happy under these conditions? I was in shock and felt alone. I read *A Day in the Life of Ivan Denisovich* and started laughing at the comparison. I found myself in America's Gulag for peace. I did this for free, and I volunteered, but this not what the Peace Corp advertises. The Peace Corps advertises the good aspects of service. The Peace Corps does not advertise your insides rotting, poor medical care, freezing on a mountain in the middle of nowhere in the name of Cold War propaganda, or their abusive country directors. False advertisement for sure.

I made tea just to stay warm as a meter of snow fell outside. I made cup after cup to stay warm, reusing the same teabag. My hands froze if they were not holding something hot and I did not want to wear gloves inside the house. Slowly my body fell apart. My hair fell out, it started graying, my eyes became dull, the bags under my eyes worsened, I aged rapidly. I did not recognize the person in the mirror. My body hurt all over. I could not feel anything. My time was spent working while my body fell apart. I had no way of contacting my family short of traveling to the nearest town and sending an email. The effect of having no contact with my family and friends took more out of me. While other Americans had internet in their homes, hot meals every night, I was by myself cut off. The nights were the worst. My only joy was staring into the fire of the wood burning stove.

I lost enthusiasm for my work as the winter grew colder. I started noting how many days until summer. Each week there was less to look forward to as I grew exhausted. I did not find anything rewarding during the week, and I searched for something. Helping kids is good work, but it became tedium in the sparse conditions. I still carried on. The college age people left the villages for work or college in the winter. My favorite spots shut down for winter. The village went indoors and stayed there. I was the only person my age in the village. I went home and made tea, and watched a movie I downloaded the previous week from the next town over. I watched the same movies over and over. My friends were on the other side of the country. I texted supportive messages every week, "You are doing important work, it's tough, but you can do this." They thanked me, it helped them out when they were going through difficult situations. Peace Corps is much more difficult than they will tell you. Still, I carried on.

Sleeping in a bag and not showering regularly caused me to have several infections. I had three infected scratches the size of nickels on my torso near my stomach. I scratched myself by accident, probably trying to dull the stomach pain. The wounds filled with puss and would not heal despite my best efforts. I grew tired of dealing with it and I no longer cared. I took a knife, heated it with a lighter, poured high grade vodka on it, shaved my chest, washed my chest, and peeled open the wounds with the knife. I peeled away the upper level of infected skin. Thick milky puss oozed out. I washed out the smelly holes in my chest one after the other. I started scrapping and cutting away any pieces of skin that could trap debris. As I went, I poured vodka on my chest which burned as my teeth clamped down. I yelled magical words into the empty apartment. Once I had dug out the wound enough, I bathed in vodka coughing all the way. Then I took the tube of *Neosporin* that I brought from America, and smeared it everywhere I could, then bandaged myself up. I reapplied the bandages and ointment daily. It healed perfectly after that. It gave me an idea to teach basic first aid to my students. I even applied the *Neosporin* to the wound of my host brother when he cut himself by accident.

I did not care anymore. I became numb to the world. I ended up having strep throat every month to the point I was downing antibiotics like candy. I called it my monthly gift. My tonsils became infected. I reported and the doctors told me to take anti-biotics month after month. They did not investigate further. I would later find out my tonsils were trapping bacteria, and I needed a tonsillectomy, which I would end up paying for a year after my service, despite the problem originating in the Peace Corps. My body was taking a beating.

After complaining for months, I had an endoscopy and an ultrasound. They noted how my gall bladder had become unusually enlarged, and the Peace Corps did nothing about it. It was causing me pain and I reported it multiple times. They found polyps and erosion of the tissue in my stomach, and did nothing. The only time the Peace Corps cares about the health of a volunteer, is when they are dead and it is on their hands. Nothing was done, so I carried on being eaten away.

The Peace Corps has the worst medical care in the United States government. Even the military was horrified when they found out what the Peace Corps was doing. The military found out the Peace Corps was still using an outdated and hazardous malaria pill that was discontinued by the military decades ago. The Peace Corps still prescribed them. The Peace Corps is slower to change than the military. That is how bad the medical care is. Volunteers have died under Peace Corps medical care, and do they take responsibility? Of course not! If you value your health, do not join the Peace Corps. Their medical care is horrible, and they know it. My gall bladder was not removed until a year after I left the Peace Corps, despite reporting it when it started causing problems. The Peace Corps does not care about the health of the volunteers, only the image. That is the point though, the Peace Corps does not want to take care of your medical problems, it is not profitable and they want the cheapest program possible. The Peace Corps treats the symptoms, and does the bare minimum to avoid legal responsibility. Then it is your problem when you are out of the Peace Corps. That is the actual policy of the Peace Corps. Treat the symptom till the volunteer is not a volunteer.

I endured all of this, and missed out on so much with my own family in friends back in the states. I still kick myself for missing my best friend's wedding. At that time, I was trying to stay warm on a mountain in the middle of nowhere. You miss out on so much while you are in the Peace Corps, but hey, you volunteered for it. I still sent a wedding gift. To say I hated life would not be true, I could not feel love or hate. I existed, working and going to bed to close my eyes till the next day started.

CHANGE OF SEASONS

Summer was wonderful, but as fall came, everything died, and winter came and turned everything to a state of grey death in Georgia. The land was a barren wasteland. The winds grew fiercer and the snow fell in large sheets. You could see the snow storms approaching over the mountains, a slow encroachment of white death. The one road higher up in the mountain was blocked until spring. Where I was, the road was taken out by a mudslide leaving everyone stuck in the village until they cleared away the debris. It became a frozen bitter cold prison for me. On top of my body losing weight from the food, I now began to freeze as I had no fat stores. My hands became skeletal, and were numb.

In school, our classes were shortened due to the lack of heat. We had 15-minute classes and I taught in my coat and boots while everyone huddled around the electric heater. The school had no internal heating and we all froze, students and teachers alike. In the winter, students learned little. I turned to kinesthetic teaching methods, like dancing and how to point out a body part when I called out the word. I focused on activities to keep kids moving to generate heat. My joints hurt more every day and my body was aging quickly. The teachers grew frustrated with the cold and the students, especially the sixth-grade class when kids are hormonal. My partner teacher grew so angry with a student, she grabbed a student's phone and threw it out the window from the second story. It landed in a snow pile. One volunteer hated dealing with his students, so he let the children fight it out in class. All volunteers become frustrated with the culture they serve in, and it comes in waves. My partner teacher grew angry with the students and reverted to corporal punishment. She forced all the students to stand in the corner on one leg. On one occasion she smacked a student across the face. That was a little shocking. I used a different method to keep them in line. I threatened to take away their monthly movie, the Georgian kids began to police each other.

DOCTOR VRACH

The responsibility of the medical failures in the Peace Corps lays firmly on the administration of the Peace Corps and their policies. I had to travel to Tbilisi via train for my medical issues. The pain in my abdomen became worrisome. I spent one weekend a month in the capital. They found polyps and other medical issues, inflammations, enlargements, strains... they issued dozens of pills, diagnosed me with nothing, and sent me back to my village. The food I was eating was causing my digestive problems, I needed surgery, but nothing was done. The doctors suggested changing my diet to include more vegetables. I spoke with my host father about it; he brought home "a" cabbage.

The Peace Corps hires local doctors from the country because they are cheaper and they know the medical system of the country. The doctor was a friendly Georgian, but they were all friendly, they were over-worked and stretched thin to the point they did not have time for anyone. The government is cheap even to the medical staff, as they had been pushing for years to get a third doctor. When I came into her office, I joked with her on medical issues and could get her laughing to the point she needed to breathe. I brought her little religious icons, and she loved it. I was the only American who brought her an icon. She was devout in her faith, and as a catholic, I respected it and we talked about the differences in our religions. She and I got along well. She was overworked, she missed several obvious diagnoses with my health, but so did the doctors in D.C. No one wanted to diagnose me with anything. They avoided any diagnoses, yet I had to have multiple surgeries once I was medically kicked out of the Peace Corps. I was in perfect health before joining. All the symptoms were there and when I talked to doctors in Ohio, they pointed to the problem immediately. They were all routine surgeries. The doctors did nothing to help me but observe.

My health was in such a poor state, I was always sick. While I was in the city undergoing an exam, I caught a fever that pushed 103 degrees. I lay in the medical hotel and rested there as my fever peaked higher and higher. The doctor came over and spent several hours with me as she monitored my condition and injected me with several drugs to try and bring the fever down. I was so cold, colder than when in the mountains. I put on every blanket I could and piled the sheets on and I lay there and endured for a long time while she sat there with me. I think she was praying, but she will never admit it. She stepped out to take a phone call every now and then, and once my fever went down, she left to go back to her office. They were swamped with dealing with so many people. She gave me instructions to stay in bed and change the sheets.

While I was laying there in the medical hotel, we talked about our lives. The Doctor was from Tbilisi, and she talked about life under the USSR. She disliked the current state of Georgia, "believe it or not, this city used to be green, trees and parks, now it is all malls." She trusted me enough to open up about her thoughts on the old ways. I held no prejudices, and was a listening spirit, I felt like a confessor. She explained, "We didn't have freedom of speech and everything was censored, but everyone had work, food, and a home. It was stable." It was an eye-opening conversation, and not one you will ever hear in America. I listened to her. I thought I was a patriot for America, I found out I was only a fanatic.

The doctor asked me what I planned to do in Tbilisi once my fever was over, "Same thing I always do, I am going to the ballet or the opera."

She was intrigued, "You don't drink with the others?" The two most common habits acquired by volunteers while in the Peace Corps are smoking and drinking.

"Why would I? Waste of money and health, I am already having stomach problems." Vrach helped me anyway she could, but due to the failure of the Peace Corps, it was little. The Peace Corps treats symptoms, much like their attempt at world peace. Nothing helped, my body continued its decay. For any serious medical problems, the foreign doctors have to report to America, and I feel as if someone from America was holding up my diagnoses. The way I was forced to live by the Peace Corps was destroying my health. Some countries have had volunteers die under the watch of Peace Corps doctors. I spent my entire service in the Peace Corps trying to find ways to ameliorate my problems, but nothing ever worked. Join the Peace Corps!

If you were curious about my patriotism, I viewed veterans akin to saints. I was raised in a military family; I looked up to them. After one of my medical examinations, I ran into the Country Director. I asked if could he deliver a small bottle of whiskey to the embassy marines for me, as a thank you for their service. One of my friends was in the Marine Corps. At the time I had thanked every veteran I met; I was proud of that. The Country Director replied, "No, because let me tell you why, I don't want those hard chargers mixing with the Peace Corps." I smiled and said I understood.

GOVERNMENT MANDATORY HOLIDAY

Thanksgiving came around, and all the volunteers were forced to meet for a conference. For the most part, it was meeting USAID officials who discussed career opportunities, and various Peace Corps administrative tasks. The USAID officials told us how great a job we were doing; we were doing their work for them. I sat in the back with the rest of the volunteers who wanted to move on with our lives. All the volunteers who wanted a government job after the Peace Corps sat up front. The Peace Corps feeds directly into any State Department or USAID job. If you have the connections, you are in. I sat beside a man who did two tours in the Peace Corps. Lisa and her friends were all near me.

The Country Director came in. His first words, "I never get tired of hearing thanks for all your hard work." We all drummed our fingers in the back. Then some guy from USAID came out. He looked and spoke like a corporate spokesman. He had a cheesy smile, a polo and khakis, connections, and earned over a hundred thousand dollars a year, plus expenses. He told us how important our work was and spoke of opportunities for future careers. They only had two spots available, and they already knew who they would select before they even made the announcement. The veteran beside me muttered, "I can smell his six-figure salary." The front row was enamored. All the volunteers in the back were playing games on our phones, on the off chance we might learn something. Those opportunities are not there, they are reserved for people with connections. On paper it is all fair and equal, but in real life, they only follow nepotism. It is like the essay section on the foreign service test; they do not state the criteria for the essay so they have leeway to choose who they want without having to explain. It has nothing to do with equality or a test, it is a way to hide nepotism. I fell asleep with my eyes open; my time was spent better that way. Their charm instantly disgusted me.

The only interesting speaker we had was a volunteer from my year. He was forced to give a speech, or be terminated. There was an incident. He was at a bar drinking and decided he wanted to start a bar fight. He grabbed a Georgian, a fatal mistake, and the rest of the Georgians threw him to the ground and stomped on his head. All Georgian men are trained in judo. The Country Director made a deal with him to avoid termination, either he gave a speech in front of everyone, or face termination. The volunteer was chain smoking after his speech, and pacing in circles like a trapped bear.

THANKLESS GIVING

The next day we had more meetings and prepared for thanksgiving dinner. I stuck close to Lisa; she was too much of a nice girl and I knew people would try and take advantage of her. We went out and bought supplies. At one point she bought vodka from a little shop. I examined the seal of the bottle, it was broken. I demanded another one, which the owner initially refused. Another volunteer told me to just take the bottle.

I turned on him, "You want to go blind? You buy it and drink it; you take the risk. That seal was broken and they could have put anything in there." Lisa saw the logic and thanked me. You have to be aware. I have heard the stories and will never trust a tampered bottle.

That night it was one big party; everyone was drinking and dancing, or doing something private in their rooms. I sat with Lisa and Soldat. Soldat was a volunteer who served twenty years in the Army before joining the Peace Corps. Soldat told me about his work over the summer in his village. His town was blazing hot in the summer and he didn't even have a fan in his cramped office. The Country Director came to visit Soldat's office and he mentioned how hot it got in his office. The Country Director's words to a twenty-year military veteran were, "Suck it up, you volunteered for this." Meanwhile the Country Director had a personal driver, a huge SUV, lived in an expensive house, his office was air-conditioned, he had a pension and a salary, all paid for by taxpayers. "Suck it up." In public he was polite and charming, behind closed doors, he was the opposite. This Peace Corps Country Director did not want *Doctors Without Borders* to come to Georgia to help the Georgians. Soldat had been working on trying to bring doctors to Georgia to help the poor who needed it, and the Country Director refused the project. He told Soldat in person, "I don't want them here, don't send an email to me, and I don't want to hear any more about this." The leaders of the Peace Corps operate behind closed doors and will refuse or deny anything that does not fit their goals. It is all an image. The Peace Corps Country Director refused to work with *Doctors Without Borders*, while a twenty-year Army Officer veteran was willing to do all the paper work and run the project. The Peace Corps refused to allow it. If the Peace Corps strives for world peace, then why all of this? Why all the opaqueness? Why is there no transparency in the Peace Corps?

Whenever anyone complained to the Country Director, he said the same thing, "You volunteered for this." This is what the Peace Corps tells volunteers to silence criticism, to prevent change. Change means the image is false and it is cheaper to be stagnant.

Volunteers will do this to other volunteers too. Volunteers silence other volunteers by calling them "whiners," and will tell them the same thing, "you volunteered for this." The volunteers from the year before us labeled my group "whiners". One highly educated volunteer from their group said it best, "complaining is how you state a problem, by being silent you let problems grow. Please, by all means, complain. Ignore them, they change nothing by being silent." Some volunteers will defer to the authority of the Peace Corps administration and silence critics, and mirror abusive directors. Some volunteers do not think independently, some just follow orders.

"You volunteered for this." No one volunteered to have their health deteriorate, to risk cancer, for women to be sexually assaulted, or any of the traumatic events the Peace Corps down plays. The Peace Corps excels in victim blaming, operating behind closed doors, and burying reports. It is the greatest bureaucratic dodge, blame the volunteers; they are volunteers after all, and no one is forcing them to be there. The Peace

Corps can always get more volunteers. The Peace Corps has a surplus of applicants, they see no reason to change. "You volunteered for this," another Peace Corps motto. No one is better at gaslighting and victim blaming than the Peace Corps.

I heard more about the Country Director chewing out a volunteer for injuring her ankle when she slipped in the mud and had to be sent away for medical treatment. The more I knew, the more I distrusted the Peace Corps. The Country Director did not even bother to learn the language as he said "I've learned so many, there's no more room," meanwhile I was searching for a tutor. The main requirement for the Peace Corps, and the Country Director was refusing to learn the Georgian language. He refused to do the most basic task required of any Peace Corps Volunteer.

One Middle-Eastern descended volunteer told me how the Country Director tried to convince her to join the CIA as she was bilingual in English and Arabic. She was a dual-citizen of America and a Middle-Eastern country. The Country Director suggested she drop the citizenship for the Middle-Eastern country and apply to the CIA as they needed Arabic speakers. He did this when they were alone at the HQ. The Peace Corps Country Director was recruiting for the CIA while in Peace Corps Georgia. Why? No one recruits for an organization they are not part of.

There is no hardline that separates the leadership of the Peace Corps, the State Department, and the CIA. They are all working together. The CIA has hired linguists from the Peace Corps, but they have to wait a few years. The Peace Corps is where the government recruits some of their linguists. There was one Returned Peace Corps Volunteer who was recruited by the CIA while working for USAID, who defected to Russia. The Returned Peace Corps Volunteer was working for USAID, when they were hired by the CIA to spy on Russia, and USAID did not know. The CIA does not notify other US agencies or departments about who is a spy. This allows them to blend in. The Peace Corps claims world peace through grass roots volunteering is the objective, and then they have a Peace Corps Country Director recruiting for the CIA. The Country Director of Georgia was working with military intelligence in Afghanistan on gathering intelligence on the Taliban before coming to lead the Peace Corps program in Georgia. The Country Director told me this himself. There are a lot of questions for the Peace Corps, and I guarantee they will not answer them honestly.

I have read reports from Peace Corps countries in South America where a country director has asked volunteers to spy for them, acting as informants. Seems there is a common trend with country directors. A Peace Corps Volunteer would make a great informant, they could do their job, send information back and not violate any laws, and be praised for their work by both countries. I sincerely doubt the CIA would plant a spy in the Peace Corps Volunteer group as a Volunteer, as anything can go wrong in the Peace Corps and it is only for two years and they would learn very little. An official spy as a volunteer would ruin the reputation of the Peace Corps if caught. JFK made the CIA swear to not plant a spy as a volunteer, they did not swear anything about the country directors, only the volunteers. However, a volunteer passing information through standard reporting would not draw suspicion. Stating which foreign people they met, just a volunteer talking about who they met, would warrant little attention. To plant an actual spy takes a bureaucrat to sign off on it, and signing off on a volunteer draws questions. Recruiting an informant draws no attention.

A country director on the other hand, would make the best spy for their position. They are a government official already, not a volunteer. They have access to all reports from volunteers, have sway on the program and can direct the Peace Corps any way they want, can find linguists, and pass information to the CIA through the embassy. They can ask volunteers to bring back information, or they can have the volunteers report on any foreign officials they meet, or have them report on any "security" concerns. A CIA spy can turn a Peace Corps program into an informant network, as the volunteers are embedded in the country, spread throughout the country, ranging from schools and villages to large scale NGOs in cities that work with governments. If they find a willing volunteer, they can place them in more important positions to influence certain projects and programs. Country Directors are there for five years minimum, nine and a half at max. Country Directors can take all the little information gathered, and process it into something valuable. It is the Country Directors that should be watched.

America has one huge language problem. The Peace Corps is a solution. A linguist in the Peace Corps has two years of intensive language training, training in cultural immersion, taught how to blend in, and gain the trust of locals. These are all the skills needed for a spy. In the Peace Corps, volunteers get their foreign relations training, pass some information along to the country director, and make connections. Once they are done in the Peace Corps, they take their benefits and apply to a government position. They end up working in the Foreign Service or any part of the government, they have their connections, and can easily become a spy later. This is how it works. Volunteers are not spies; at most they are informants working for a spy who would be the country director. They may be spies later, as it has happened with Returned Peace Corps Volunteers before. If you want to be a spy, join the Peace Corps.

The assistant country directors, they are usually focused on working with the Peace Corps back in DC and maintaining the communication lines and keeping everyone one on track with Peace Corps goals. The country director is focused on the project in the country and working with the embassy and managing relations in country. There are American accountants in the Peace Corps, but they have little contact with anyone and their position needs a high level of accounting experience.

One country director recruiting for the CIA in Georgia with a history of working with military intelligence, and another country director in South America recruiting informants; seems too much to be a coincidence. Obviously not all Peace Corps programs would be involved in spy networks, that is too much. Georgia is however right beside Russia and Iran, and America's foreign policy is to contain Russia and Iran. In Africa, they need the foreign people believing America cares about them, that is the epicenter of the Peace Corps image. However, in China, the language training is six months, double that of the standard language training, and it is obvious to see the government wants Chinese speaking Americans, and spreading pro-American sentiment in China. Need Arabic? Morocco. The Peace Corps is a wonderful multi-purpose tool, turning college kids into informants, linguists, diplomats, making them something useful to the American Government, and influencing foreigners. It has always been this way; JFK wanted the volunteers to move into the Foreign Service since the beginning. Those foreigners that volunteers helped, can now be more easily influenced by the American Government. One student of a volunteer went on to be a president of a country. Influence is the goal of the Peace Corps.

AMBASSADOR OF TURKEY

Volunteers did the cooking. We were excited to meet the Ambassador who was joining us for Thanksgiving dinner. The Country Director wanted everything to be perfect. The Ambassador and the Country Director were polar opposites. I was caught off-guard by the Ambassador. He had a low-key personality, surprisingly down to earth. He was a Midwestern academic, and felt genuine. The Country Director, he felt like two people in one, and the one you spoke with was trying to hide the other. The Ambassador's wife was equally as laidback as the Ambassador, and they acted like any couple from the Midwest. I was not expecting that. He and his wife carved the turkey and served the volunteers, and had a bunch of photos taken.

I had the ambassador's wife cracking up when I went to grab some turkey. Being from the Midwest and an academic, I threw a few jokes that had her laughing. I caught her off guard. I did a comedy routine for a minute and then snagged some turkey and left her laughing. They struck me as good people, even if the only thing they did was show up, carve a turkey, take a photo, eat and skedaddle. Why was the Country Director so stressed by the Ambassador's presence? Without knowing more, it seemed like the difference between midwestern genuineness and diplomatic façade.

SHAKE DOWN

During the conference, Druggie, another volunteer, and I decided to explore Tbilisi. It was a cool day. We went to a museum to check out some of the art of Georgia and then decided to grab lunch at a restaurant. The three of us were walking through a park to the restaurant at two in the afternoon. Druggie by this point had not done any form of intoxicant for years, and I call him that as a joke, he is a clean professional man. We all were. Two Georgian police officers drove up, pulled up beside us, got out, stopped us, grabbed Druggie's backpack and threw it in the backseat of the squad car and told us to empty our pockets. They were talking rapidly in Georgian, faster than normal, trying to intimidate us. We emptied our pockets, having nothing on us and having come to serve their country in the Peace Corps. Druggie called it out, "It's a shake down."

We identified ourselves as English Teachers in the Peace Corps in their language, and then they spoke a mile a minute in a demanding voice, we asked them to slow down so as to understand, they did not. They patted us down. I checked with a lawyer friend of mine from Georgia, and this is an illegal search even in their country. They found a tiny knife on a pair of nail clippers on Druggie, the blade the size of the tip of your pinky finger, so small you could clean your ear with it. In English they told me and the other volunteer we could go. They grabbed Druggie and started to turn their backs on us to put him in the squad car. The other volunteer moved a little bit; I do not know if he was trying to leave or readjusting his stance, I saw him move in the corner of my eye as I was looking directly at the cops. That put Druggie's words into a concrete perspective. They were using intimidation and divisive tactics to isolate my friend. I had to take command of the situation. They were crooked cops trying to shake money out of Peace Corps Volunteers who came to help their country.

"No, we are one." I said in Georgian, that sentence being easy to remember in their language. I switched to English and said out loud to reassure my friend and to tell the other volunteer the plan, "If one of us goes to jail, we all go to jail." The cops turned and looked at me surprised to see I did not turn and run. I smelled uncertainty in them and I starred them down as I grabbed my phone to call the Security Manager at the Peace Corps office. The Peace Corps has a person connected with the local police to facilitate any legal situations.

I told the security manager what was going on while the cops were saying something to me and the other American, I ignored them without breaking eye contact and handed the phone to the police officer saying, "American Government, speak." They wanted to treat us like crap, I will talk to them like dogs. The police officer refused to take the phone and threw Druggie's backpack at him. Then they quickly hopped in their car and took off. I was pissed. Here we were, coming to help Georgia, spending our health and time to help them and their cops were trying to shake money out of us using intimidation tactics. We were walking in a park and were searched with no justification in the middle of the day. There is no excuse for their abject failure of conduct. Expect this in the Peace Corps, you are an American, all you represent is money, and even foreign cops will harass volunteers. I told the Peace Corps Security Manager I would file a report.

"Thanks for not abandoning me, I was getting ready to spend a night in jail again." Druggie said.

"No one fights alone, if you go to jail, we all go to jail." We continued on our way to the restaurant.

When I spoke with the Security Manager, the Peace Corps official responsible for the security of the volunteers, she refused to take any official report, and when I pressed the issue, she walked away. The Peace Corps actively refuses to take reports. All she did was defend the Georgian police who were trying to isolate my friend to do whatever they wanted. "Georgian police don't harass tourists and don't do shake downs; they were trained by American police. What were you doing?" A Peace Corps Security Manager victim blamed us and called us tourists. We were walking from a museum to a restaurant through a park in the middle of the day while serving in the Peace Corps.

She refused to take a written report and refused to take any further action even when I mentioned their body cameras and how easy it would be to track them down. She refused to take any more action saying the Georgian police are trained to not target tourists and then she walked away from me, denying everything that happened. I told her we are not tourists, but she refused to do anything. That told me the Peace Corps does not care, and even the employees of the Peace Corps consider the volunteers to be tourists, and they refuse to take reports over blatant security violations and targeting by the police. We were not tourists, we were Peace Corps Volunteers, and once again, proof the Peace Corps only cares about its image, even when their own volunteers are being targeted by police.

The police were threatening to take my friend away, and I had to stare them down. Nothing in the Peace Corps manual mentions this. If you join the Peace Corps, be prepared to stare down foreign cops in their own capital. This is what you will face in the Peace Corps. The local police will intimidate and use scare tactics to get money out of you, and you came to help their children. These are cops from Tbilisi, and yes, Georgia should be ashamed of them. Your safety does not matter in the Peace Corps. The Peace Corps will not protect you, and they will silence you, they will bury reports in favor of their image. The reality of the Peace Corps goes against the Peace Corps image.

Reporting anything in the Peace Corps is useless. The Peace Corps actively buries reports in country, and when reports get back to DC, they bury them there. The Peace Corps has reports, but hides them. For a court case, the Peace Corps was requested to release documents about the safety of volunteers. The Peace Corps used the excuse that it would cost too much to compile reports, when in reality, they already had them. What the Peace Corps fears is losing their "image" which is all it is. Once the image is gone, it is nothing but a foreign affairs bureaucracy. There is no altruism in the Peace Corps. The real problem is the side effect of hiding the truth, as that denial fosters stagnation and jeopardizes the health and welfare of the volunteers.

WHERE HOME IS A DIRTY WORD

The following month we had to meet up with the Country Director for a planned emergency evacuation drill, just in case the Russians came back. All regions had to conduct one, so every volunteer in our region met up at a pre-designated location. Then we all went to lunch together. I had the fun of sitting with the Security Manager and the Country Director, and a few other volunteers.

The conversation was about local places and everyone was talking about where they had been, sight-seeing wise. I was speaking to the Georgians about the local churches I visited and prayed at, and many of them were beautiful and I said so. Small, but well-built and beautiful in an austere way. The Georgians looked touched that I had taken the time to pray at their Holy places and admired their religious work, especially their Cathedral in Tbilisi. The Country Director spoke from across the table, "You should see the cathedrals in Italy, those are the most beautiful on earth. All are ornate and every inch is decorated. Just absolutely beautiful. Especially the one in Florence."

I smiled awkwardly; I have a minor in medieval studies and had climbed to the top of the Duomo while I was in college. "I've been to them." The conversation fell flat, as his one-upmanship killed the conversation. I was praising the Georgians on their cultural and religious heritage and explaining how I was incorporating their culture into my faith, and he started talking about the beauty of another country. I smiled awkwardly.

The conversation moved onto plans for Christmas and the winter break. Many volunteers were travelling for Christmas. We had a total of 48 days off for the full two years, and many volunteers were planning on going home for the holiday, or to Egypt, France, wherever. The Country Director told us he was going to be with his family in Amsterdam for the New Year. He asked me what I planned. "I plan to go back home to see friends and family for Christmas."

He jumped up in his seat pointing his finger at me, then barked an order/threat at me, "You go to America, you stay there! Stay in your village." Instantly I was crushed. Not only could I not see my family for the holidays, I could not even travel to neighboring countries for a weekend. I had not seen my family for a long time. I could only email my family once a week at best. I was perhaps one of the most isolated there, as the rest of the volunteers I met had internet in their homes. I had to travel to the next town over to use the internet. I felt even more alone now. I would be the only American in the mountains for Christmas as all other volunteers in my area were leaving. I would have to experience Christmas alone on a mountain.

My Christmas vacation to see my family was cancelled on the whim of a bureaucrat. Meanwhile the Country Director spent the holiday with his family, paid for by taxpayers. I was forced by the Peace Corps to miss Christmas with my family when it was not even necessary. The schools took the same winter break as Americans. I would be sitting alone in my village. No other volunteers were blocked from travelling, he was targeting me. Why? Volunteers have to apply to leave on vacation and register their itinerary. The Country Director has the final say in who is allowed to leave. I was not allowed to use my vacation tome during my vacation, and instead I was forced to work on Christmas, a federal holiday. While you are in country, you are on the job. Country Directors are abusive bullies.

I have no idea why he reacted the way he did, or why he was targeting me. I know one thing about the Peace Corps, one word they watch for, in terms of assimilation, is the word "Home". Only in the Peace Corps is home a dirty word. If the Peace Corps catches you using the word home for America and not your village, they use it against you in judging your assimilation. There are no homes in the Peace Corps. At the end of the meeting, the Country Director told me, while everyone else was out of ear shot, in a pathetic excuse for a face-saving gesture with a fake smile, "Trust me, you'll want to see how Georgian's celebrate New Year's." Then he got in his SUV and left. I had planned to be back by December 29th. Every volunteer was told how important New Year's is for Georgians in training. None of my friends or family celebrate New Year's in America. He just decided for fun to ruin my holiday.

CRAZY IVANA

My time serving could be summed up in relation to one crazy partner teacher. Crazy Ivana, she was obsessed with America. She had been there on one of the American government's funded tours, and wanted to return and live there her whole life. She hated her life in Georgia; where many men drink and cheat on their wives, while the women are stuck working and raising a family. Who wouldn't want to run away? Even I would be made fun of for doing the dishes and being respectful to women. She was married and her husband had cheated on her with a Muscovite right after she gave birth to his child. By the time I met her, she was in her early thirties and had kids. Her husband worked, but he wanted to be a normal villager.

She married out of societal pressure and wanted to escape to the American utopia and leave all her troubles behind. I did my best to convince her not to chase that dream and face reality. I did the kindest thing I could for her, I gave her Hobson's Choice, "Alright, I'll tell you what, leave your family behind, your children, your husband, and marry me. I'll take you to America." A Georgian mother would never abandon her children. For three months she fought with herself over it, but I knew her better than she knew herself. She confessed this to me when her husband was not around; for three months, every night she would tuck her children into bed, and in the back of her mind she fought with herself about what was more important. She was a good mother from the start, I knew it, we all knew it, her husband knew it, only she did not. She yelled at me later.

"Poo on you! I used to dream of coffee in New York. Now I dream about a new toilet. You are Devil! Why?"

I laughed, "You needed to face reality and stop dreaming of running away to America. The American government wants you to want them. It's a pipe dream, and pipe dreams like pipe bombs explode. I knew you would never leave your children, your husband sure, but you would never abandon your children. I wanted you to know you cannot run to America. If you want to go, it will take years of making your life better here, and you can apply once your life is better." She no longer thought about running, and then she took that energy and focused on improving herself as a teacher and her life in the present. It was the kindest thing I could have done for her. We grew stronger in our friendship.

I started to work on her English. She kept pronouncing the word boat, "Bow-At." We spent so much time together, her English started to mirror mine. She started to dream in English; she was frustrated as she started to forget her own language. We spent all day teaching together, then at night, we met up once again to lesson plan. It was a relentless cycle of teaching and planning and it was exhausting. If she had a question, she asked me. I explained translations and grammar and every possible facet of any word, no matter the word. If she ever asked for help, I was there. I helped her apply for international programs. When she told me she wanted to build a small library where she could teach after school, outside of school, I sat down and started planning. My contribution to Peace Corps Georgia was going to be refurbishing an abandoned apartment into a small library. I sent out dozens of emails for book donations and started putting together my proposal. This was going to be my big Peace Corps project.

YETI AND GHOST

To lesson plan with Ivana, I had to march a mile on a mountain road every night, through the winter with meter high snow in the dark. I bundled up in my heavy boots and heavy overcoat and marched on her house. I am thankful for the boots I bought; I spent extra on my footwear before I left America, knowing I was going into the post-Soviet winter. The best boots I ever owned, perfect for ice-marching through the winter in the Peace Corps. The fangs of winter could not frostbite. Ivana was worried I would be hit by a car so she slapped a reflective patch on my backpack and had me call her when I made it back home. The roads were dangerous and so were the drunk drivers. Every night I did this. By the time I got home, my beard was covered in ice and snow caked my coat and pants. As I walked, chunks of snow fell off me. I left around ten at night, and came back after midnight. Many times, I had to get out of bed, then march through the ice and snow when she needed help or wanted to vent. I left my room as a Peace Corps Volunteer and came back a Yeti.

It was pitch black on that road at night, a sheer drop into darkness on one said, and a mountain face on the other. The only light was my shifty dinky plastic flashlight. When a car approached, I made sure to face the beam in whatever direction the car was coming from to signal my presence. I stepped off the road a meter, careful not to fall off the side. Ivana worried every night that I would be hit by a car.

I could think clearly on that road, no one around. The only light besides that in my hand was the moon and stars. Moonlight cast shadows fiercely in the darkness, and I felt at home, alone in the dark, only myself. I sometimes stopped and sat and looked at the stars, seeing the universe and the night sky clearly for the first time in my life. Away from the city, on a mountain, and in pitch black, the sky never looked clearer. I could hear the wind howl and cut through the valley. I was happiest here in the dark and the cold outside, it was a nurturing numbness. I turned my torch off and waited, listening to the wind and watching the dalliance of the stars. It reminded me of *Pokémon* cards, the old holographic ones. The only peace I found was out in the cold alone.

At one point I heard movement through snow and under the dead brush. I turned the light on realizing I was not alone. Most of the time it was some rodent heading to its burrow, a group of jackals, maybe feral dogs. I could hear them and they ran near me, but never at me. The large Yeti holding the light scared them away. They never scared me. The only time I was scared was when one of the streets dogs jumped out at me from the darkness. My blood turned as cold as the water in the river below me. It was a pure white German Shepard. All white, it had been sleeping in the snow, and when it saw me, it jumped out to play excitedly. This dog was friendly and walked with me in the Summer, and followed Lisa as she jogged, we fed him together. We named it Ghost. Imagine it, pitch black, no sound, a tiny flashlight, snow falling and boom, teeth and black lips darting at you from your peripheral vision, right out of the snow. It did not bite, it wanted to play. After I stress laughed, I tossed a few snowballs for it to chase. It loved catching snowballs in its teeth. It waited for me every night in winter near the village in the snowbanks, waiting for the Yeti to come play. I walked with the Ghost dog in that valley.

Even when my flashlight failed and I was left to wonder in the dark, I could still make my way home on a full moon night. I could not see one foot in front of me when there was no moon. I followed the road by footfall or by-passing car light. Eventually making it home to my dreary room. I was happier in the snow vale under the stars in the dark than my own bed. I sat out there in the dark sometimes and breathed the crystal clean air. I sometimes wrote a note of a poem long since lost. I miss the snow vale, watching my own breath in the moonlight, seeing the clouds cast shadows in the darkness over the frozen river. Watching the moon sit far over the mountains, frozen trees. In ice, I was frozen with joy, it was clean and no one bothered me, save the white beast begging me to throw a snowball.

Some nights Ivana stayed up late tutoring for extra pay and then she would call me and I would climb out from under my mountain of blankets, lace up my boots and begin the ice-march. In those nights, when we were planning lessons, it was us joking and laughing. Those moments became intimate. We never crossed any lines, but we grew close, she was a few years older than me, but we chimed on many levels. I loved her kids too. Her daughter, who was three going on four, was insanely jealous of me taking her mother away from her. I had to pay attention to her too, only then could we work. Some of those nights the power went out, and it was us laughing by fire joking about English words. I do not think there were any closer partners in the Peace Corps, at least in Georgia. She cooked on special occasions, macaroni and cheese, a pizza. We had tea together most nights. Her house was heated by a massive wood burning stove. I scraped the ice off my coat and sat in the warmth of the company and the fire. Her husband knew we were close, but we all knew we would not do anything.

She was sad when I went away for medical evaluations in Tbilisi. I always brought something back for her or her family. I raided the Free Table every time I was there. I went in with an empty bag and took everything. I grabbed sports shirts, nice dresses, and anything of value. I gave those to Ivana who would give them to other women in the village or her family. I found cameras, smartphones, sleeping bags, boots, backpacks, suitcases, and at one point a guitar. I took everything and redistributed to friends and volunteers who needed them. They labeled it free for anyone, and I was anyone. I gave a camera to the school, boots to another volunteer who did not have anything save sneakers in winter in the mountains. One phone went to another American in need, and clothes to anyone who needed them. The smartphones I gave to Ivana to give to her family. Her family loved me. She was trying to find a cousin for me to marry, but it never panned out.

Her family brought me along for family events. Dinners, trips, funerals, weddings, I was their American cousin. All her sisters loved me for my generosity, dedication, and humor. My work and relentless ice-marches were noticed by everyone. I looked forward to those nights where I could be myself and I could have her laughing and her kids giggling. She said I would be a good father one day. Her sisters thought so too. Her nephew was nineteen and had a good mind on his shoulders, he had a sense of humor 1.6 kilometers wide. We got along great. One night we were all hanging out in Batumi, I was spending the weekend with her family. Her nephew and I slept in a spare room without any heating in winter. I ended up sleeping in my boots, my coat, and under massive blankets piled on me. We did not sleep. We spent the night giggling over stupid jokes like we were kids in the third grade while freezing our butts off. He was like my childhood best friend all those years ago. Misery loves company. We joked about the wealthiest family's son in our village, the one who challenged me on the beach. I called him a smart idiot, the nephew started laughing, "That is perfect for him."

We spent the next day pigging out on pizza and ice cream in Batumi. Being part of their family helped keep me going despite everything I was enduring. I started opening up more. It was like laughing in the third grade. I did not care and laughed at the darkest jokes imaginable. Georgians have a dark sense of humor; it matched their stressful lives. Georgians laugh to conquer their own lives. I laughed with them. I spent many evenings helping her apply to different travel programs to America, nothing panned out, but I still did my most for her and her family.

PULING A CRAZY IVAN WITH CRAZY IVANA

The craziest time was at the partner teacher conferences. In the volunteer's first year, all volunteers had to go with their partner teacher to conferences in hotels in the off season to learn project management and other basic skills. Ivana loved going to these and seeing which volunteers were sleeping with who, she was disappointed by my year. The first conference was in Batumi. We spent the night with her family, hopped a bus, and ended up at the hotel. We showed up, walked around seeing the frozen shore, all bundled up in winter clothing, hearing the crash of icy waves. We went inside to grab dinner. I sat with her and her friends which were other Georgian women, and proceeded to have the table laughing with outrageous jokes.

After dinner I walked Ivana to her room and chatted with her. She started smoking. She rebelled against her culture by smoking in the hotel room. Georgian conservative culture would label her a "bad girl" if she was seen doing anything remotely immoral. Georgian culture is hard on Georgian women. She was forced to be a good girl. For her, smoking was defiance.

I went back to my room and for the first time in years, I poured myself a bath. Hot water poured out, and I took my cut up and scarred up body, and lay down in the hot water and soaked. I removed the bandages covering my wounds. My bones cracked as I climbed in. I sank beneath the miniature waves. I sat there in the warmth and relaxed for the first time since summer, after my body had taken a monumental beating. I soaked for several hours fully submerging myself in the gargantuan bathtub. My body felt broken, and it was knitting itself together in the warm water. I washed out my wounds and rested. I drained the tub and refilled it several times so I was not soaking in filth. The first time I drained the tub, the water was grey. My body was covered in acne from all the oil. I sank beneath the water with only my nose above. It was the most relaxing bath I ever had. I propped my head up and fell asleep in the warmth.

Mjolnir was my roommate and he was playing video games while I soaked. I put on my robe and walked over to sit beside Mjolnir in bed, we had a queen together. We joked as he turned on the TV. I threw him his robe and he thanked me as he put it on. Two guys, sitting together in robes in a queen size bed, that is how you know you have reached bromance. We turned on the tv to a fashion show with models on the catwalk. We sang *I'm Too Sexy* as we watched the model's strut. I turned on my commentary and had him laughing at my shenanigans. "White after Labor Day? No, no, take it back to the drawing board, these designs are all wrong. Is he even wearing pants?" We relaxed all evening cracking the dumbest jokes about fashion as we sat in bed together.

The conference was boring and mind numbing. Dumbed down activities for busy work where one hour might buy a minute of worthy information, good return on investment. Ivana sat right beside me and we whispered stupid jokes to each other. We pulled a few pranks together. We staged photos where it looked like we were fighting, but the conversation was about types of toilet paper, including the Russian one that is effectively sandpaper. At lunch time and at breaks I discovered the hotel kept putting out tea if the tea box emptied. At the end of every break, I dumped the box in my backpack, and then went back to the conference. I walked out with a trash bag full of tea, most of which I gave away. Mjolnir was laughing when I offered him tea at night.

I did something that shocked everyone at the conference. I bought an hour-long massage for Ivana at the spa room in the hotel. I felt bad for her, she worked like a dog raising her family, working twelve-hour days, and I thought she deserved a break, it was my Christmas gift to her. I took her down to the spa, dropped a chunk of change, and left. She needed it. Many other Georgian teachers were jealous. The Georgian managers even commented, I noticed with a slight envy in their tone, "That's a really generous gift." I told them she was my friend, and she deserved more as I felt bad for her, that and it was for the children as she worked incredibly hard. They took note of my successful adaptation and working relationship with her. I do not think there were any closer partners in Peace Corps Georgia, but that is hard to say. We had a close bond, Ivana and I, and everyone could see it. She was so relaxed after the massage and told me not to tell anyone back in the village for fear everyone would think we were sleeping together. We were not of course, I viewed the mission as the most important thing, and she had two wonderful children.

Ivana made me face palm when she told me she thought the Turkish masseuse was ugly. She said a few off-color comments. When we were talking about China in class, she turned to me, pulled her eye lids to the side to narrow them, and went, "Ching-chon-ding-dong," in front of the class. The asinine behavior was strong with this one. I worked hard on improving her global view.

During one of the breaks, an idiot volunteer was running around showing a video he found funny. He showed me the video he took of a cow being slaughtered in his village. The farmers tied it up, then chopped the cows head off. The volunteer laughed harder and harder as blood spurt out and the animal died. His delight in the cow's death disturbed me. I still remember the tears in his eyes as he laughed. I was not disturbed about the cow dying, I am from Ohio and know this happens, it is nothing to laugh at though. I left the idiot behind and sat down with Druggie who was sitting in the far corner by himself, he had a cup of tea with him while he watched the rest of the room. "Did you see the video..." He nodded as he looked in the direction of the idiot volunteer. Druggie's observations were always fun, he called me a mad genius. Best compliment I ever got while in the Peace Corps.

That night Druggie and I went to the pool room. Later Ivana joined us. We all talked for a while. She told me about the massage and how great she felt as we floated in the pool. She was a trapped woman; I could see it, a liberal woman in a conservative culture. I knew the look, the want to escape anyway possible. It is a screwed-up world. We talked of our lives, and how she loved swimming more than anything. I floated with her and, our heads bumped into each other. We talked openly for a good long time. Water gave her freedom.

After about an hour we headed to the sauna where a massive Russian man covered in tattoos and muscles was sitting. It was the Russian, Druggie, and me sitting in silence together...in manly silence. The silence was broken by the idiot volunteer and his friends who came in chattering like imbeciles. The idiot started pouring water on the hot rocks, steaming it up till complete saturation. He poured the water fifteen times. He finally stopped when the Russian spoke, "That is good." The idiot stopped dead in his tracks with a look of horror on his face. Druggie and I looked at each other. It was a nice dry heat before, now it was saturated. The Russian walked out into the outdoor pool in freezing weather to swim, then came back into the sauna and repeated this process for the next hour. This was clearly not a man to mess with. The idiot who kept pouring water on the hot rocks, was one of the idiots who was getting drunk in training. I stayed away from him.

DANCE PARTY

That evening Ivana invited me to the conference room. The Georgian teachers had turned it into a dance hall. They commandeered the projector and sound system, and played a dancing video game. These women danced full throttle. I joined in, as best I could with my stiff ankle and back. That is when I met her. I only talked a few times with her in passing. Anastasia, she was Ivana's roommate and friend. I sat across from her at dinner a few times and joked with her and Ivana. She had a beautiful smile. I can remember her dancing; she was graceful. For our one dance together, we lived step by step for that moment.

I can still remember her in her blue jeans and sweater. She was tall and voluptuous, a perfect build of feminine strength and beauty. She was a few years older than me. She had the perfect hourglass in which we danced our time away that evening. I could smell her when she danced close to me, nothing but intoxicating. I am sure I was exuding body odor. She smiled a pure enrapturing smile. This was a woman who loved passion, and went for what she wanted. She found a man who could make her laugh, and listened to her when she spoke. We danced in perfect unison, our legs meeting step for step and it was the most passionate dance of my life. We looked into each other's eyes, her oaken eyes, a beautiful brown. I saw an immense sadness in her eyes but a love for life in that moment. It was the most passionate three minutes of my life. After the dance, we sat beside each other, talking as others danced. The night ended and we parted for our respective rooms as we were tired and had another day of seminars.

The next day was a blur of boring seminars and projects. All through the courses Anastasia and I made faces at each other from across the room, and other jokes. At lunchtime and breaks we cracked each other up while I pocketed al the tea I could. Ivana was shaking her head laughing, I felt she was a little jealous. That was the last day of the seminar, and we had to return to our lives. I met up with Ivana at the hotel desk. Anastasia walked by, "Goodbye American boy", she said as she walked by, she bumped me with her hip as she walked away.

Ivana came over, "She's married."

"Well, that's frustrating." We returned to our villages where Ivana told me not to speak of the hotel.

CHRISTMAS OF SUCK

It was cold and bitter. All the volunteers in my area left for vacation or to their respective hometowns back in America. All of the American Peace Corps staff left as well. I was the only American in the mountains. On Christmas day I went to town to see my Georgian friends. I did not want to be alone. I was miserable. I broke down in front of my Georgian friend when she wished me a "happy Christmas." She ran over and hugged me. I thanked her. The first Christmas away is the worst, isolated while everyone else is together. You will never feel more alone. You have to make your own holiday wherever you are, and you have to be with people you love, or else it will be miserable.

The only good thing that happened was that I was able to meet a few older volunteers for a Christmas toast in Batumi. It was a last-minute thing, a small get-together for any volunteers still in the region. I fit in better with the mature volunteers. One of the older women felt my arm up and asked, "Give me a flex, I am an old woman." I obliged her groping hand, despite some minor complaints in the back of my mind. After the party, I was able to use the internet and talk with my family thanks to the host. She joined us for the Christmas family teleconference. She was hit hard this Christmas due to a nasty divorce that led her to the Peace Corps. She was an amazing human being. She was happy to be invited and my family was happy to meet another volunteer, and a good one.

They were happy to hear from me. There was some comfort from that, and some comedy in my grandmother calling Stalin, "Uncle Joe", a name used by America during World War Two. I was happy to see friends and family for at least an hour or two.

Returning to my home in the village was the most depressing memory I have from the Peace Corps. Forced to live a Christmas away from family, blocked from even going on vacation with other volunteers. Peace Corps Country Directors have far too much authority. Americans do not have rights in the Peace Corps. The Country Director operates behind closed doors and if he wants to get rid of you, he will find a way. The Peace Corps' rules are so vague as to allow themselves any reason to get rid of someone, and there is a long history of it. They do not need a reason to terminate volunteers their first year of service, it has happened before, and it will happen again.

There is no excuse for ordering someone to miss Christmas. I was an English teacher, a position of no importance on Christmas break. The government was not even paying for my plane ticket, that was my own money I had saved, and I had vacation time that I was denied. English teacher volunteers are only allowed to use their vacation time in summer and on Christmas break, and I was denied even that. Orthodox religions do not celebrate Christmas on the 25th of December, they celebrate in January. I was planning to be back for New Year's so as not to miss the holiday in my country of service, I would have missed nothing. The Country Director did not care. Put that in the advertisements for the Peace Corps, "Miss Christmas with your family because a Peace Corps Country Director threatened to kick you out, meanwhile he was in Amsterdam with his family."

NEW YEAR'S EVE

I had missed out on being with my family, and I no longer cared about a hypocritical Peace Corps Country Director. I spent my holiday serving America, he did not. I celebrated New Years in a way I wanted. I took off to Batumi and hit a bazar on a mission to buy New Year's gifts. I hopped off the bus and into the crowded, cramped, and wet bazar and started haggling. That night I gave my gift to my host father a very nice backgammon board. My host father gave me an empty wine bottle, I thanked him and used it as a flower vase. He loved his board.

Before midnight, I went out into the streets as all the teenagers were preparing high powered fireworks. One teen jokingly aimed one of the rockets at me. I ducked out of the way and headed over to Maria's house. Maria and her family were standing on the balcony. Her father was drunk dancing on the couch listening to the Russian broadcast of New Year's music, dancing to some Euro song. I stood with Maria as her brother put an arm around me and her grandpa rested his head on my shoulder and we watched the night turn to day as the sky filled with rockets at midnight. I thought to myself about how the times have changed. Under the burning night sky, we were a family enjoying New Year's together. With Maria's family, I was at home. We ate and drank that night. I drank arm in arm with the old red army grandpa.

The next day I boarded a train in Batumi. I told myself the eternal words, "Fuck it, I'm living my life." I took off to see my volunteer friends scattered across the country, the ones who stayed. School did not start again till the middle of the month and all of the American Peace Corps staff were gone. Off I went, only telling the volunteers I wanted to see. I still turned in my where-abouts via text every night, a must do in case of emergency, and they only check in case of emergency. No one cared, as there was no one to check, and no emergency.

On the train I watched the snowfall on a picturesque world of ice and snow over soviet ruins. I thought to myself as I travelled, "How much more of a person you become when you take risks, and go at it on your own? Is that what being a man is? A human?" Embracing free will is empowering, as opposed to obeying your whole life as I had till this point. I had embraced free will. Once I reached the capital, I headed to my cheap hotel. Lisa called me and we met up. We went off on a history tour. We headed to the museums, tourist sites, and to the old bazar where they sold soviet antiques. There I helped Lisa buy a few items, and a few gifts for family in America. We prayed at a couple of churches on our journey.

We only stopped to eat fattening Georgian street food, Khachapuri; it was delicious. It fueled our march up a mountain, Mtastminda. We climbed for two hours up a winding path; it was a small mountain travelled well. We climbed to the top. Once there, we laughed about falling to our deaths as we sat on the edge of a cliff face on a bench that jutted out over the fall. She laughed, "I hope this holds." We found some of those tourist binoculars and used them to spy over the city. We trekked off to a restaurant where we chowed down a nice plate of Khinkali, Georgian dumplings, and by the night's end we took off to our cheap hotel. We spent the night eating smoked sausage and reminiscing about the 90's. Back then, the greatest threat to the American government was *Eminem*, we laughed, simpler times. We passed out around midnight after hiking an estimated ten miles that day.

We woke up and caught a taxi to her city. Once there, she showed me around, introduced me to people, telling me who was a corrupt. We walked around, seeing odd statues, places where she went for runs in the morning. She showed me where she found two Georgian teenagers going at it hard, early one morning on her run; she turned and ran the other way. We found our way into old soviet ruins where we ate bean bread together, Lobiani. When we left, we walked through the streets of the town and bumped into two Neo-Nazis, skinheads complete with armbands. We kept walking, ignoring them and proceeded to joke about them, "You do realize the Soviets won, right? Like your great grandpa beat them? You're rooting for the losers." There were Nazis even in Georgia. We returned to her home to meet her family. I had dinner with them. Lisa and I slept in the same bed, as there were no other options and we were freezing.

The next day I hopped a bus to the edge of the country as Lisa had a project to attend to. I soldiered on to Soldat's town, crossing the entire country. He found a hotel for me. We spent the days talking about our lives, and what he did on his daily routine in his town. He worked hard to help his family and community here. We walked around seeing monuments to the Red Army. We joked and hiked through the woods. We hiked so much; night fell before we realized what time it was. We stood by a dried-up riverbed as we talked about geology as the sun set. I was the first to visit him in his town.

He talked about the stresses he had all stemming from the Country Director. He had a list of projects and plans all kiboshed by the glorious leader of peace because. The Country Director did not want to deal with any new projects. He wanted everyone to do their basic job and nothing more. Our glorious leader wanted an easy job and to collect his salary, he did not care about helping the people we came to help. The Peace Corps Country Director said no to bringing in *Doctors Without Borders*. Who says no to that? The Country Director told Soldat to not send any emails to him on the subject either, he did not want to leave any fingerprints anywhere. He was a slippery bureaucrat.

Soldat was the most honest and genuine man on the face of the earth, dedicated to his cause, a patriot, a veteran, and a human being focused on helping other human beings. Soldat was the truest Peace Corps Volunteer I ever met. He used his own money to support his host family, and helped provide a better education for his host brother. He wanted to make sure his host brother, a kid of sixteen, did not become a village alcoholic. Soldat planned to use his own money to take his host brother on a trip to Greece, to get him to see the world and that there is more to the world. His host family approved. The Country Director refused and implied that Soldat was a pedophile, stating something about trafficking a minor across international borders for sex. I was not there for that, as the Country Director operates behind closed doors. Soldat said out loud, "The Country Director can go fuck himself, insinuating I'm a pedophile." He had his host family's permission, and only needed the Peace Corps to say ok to a travel education. He got called a pedophile for it by the Peace Corps. He did multiple tours, served his country faithfully in the military his whole life, and did multiple tours in the Peace Corps. He was the most patriotic person I ever met. There is no excuse for the Country Director. I thanked Soldat for his service. He spent his own money to educate the locals around him and helped teach them to be self-sufficient and independent. Meanwhile his country refused his work. I grew disillusioned with the Peace Corps.

That night we had a hot cooked meal in a beer hall. A great meal for sure, drinking beer, we kicked back over Khinkali. I see why Soldat fights so hard, despite what he had to deal with. He was a role model of the highest caliber, a strong man. He was proficient at everything he did, and studied Georgian religiously, one of the few who believed in the linguistic mission of the Peace Corps. In the morning we had tea and breakfast, and walked through the woods and soviet ruins. We hugged goodbye as I had to go on my travels again, as I was trying to hit all my friends over the break. I was the first of my year to visit friends so far away, to travel the full length of the country, border to border.

Druggie's home was a beautiful little house in a forgotten city. We went hiking through old soviet factories and across old bridges that were ready to collapse. We spent the night in in his house, eating, freezing, talking about life. All of us were run down by our first year, and were facing exhaustion, deteriorating morale, and becoming burnt out. They were all happy I came to visit. I messaged them every few weeks to boost morale and check in on them, trying to be as supportive as possible. "Remember, I am with you, and you're work means something.

I know it's hard, but do it for the glory of...oh to hell with it, you can do it!" They would message me back and thank me for the support. My messages meant more to them than I knew. A reminder they were not alone. Everyone is isolated in the Peace Corps. Everyone was isolated and burnt out on empathy and volunteer work. Soon enough I returned to my village, and back to my chilly life of potatoes.

I felt happier that I had gone out on my own and enjoyed my time, supporting friends, bringing news, gifts, stories, and all sorts of joy that a rogue friend brings on his wayward visit during an isolated holiday. Even when I went rogue, I was still doing work to support the mission of the Peace Corps and the Volunteers. Let the Peace Corps argue about that; did I apply for time off or vacation on this holiday? No, I had no work to do, and the Country Director was an unreliable leader. I still turned in my where-abouts by text. I could not trust the leader of the Peace Corps.

CONFERENCE 2: MORAL FRUSTRATION

My stomach pain was growing worse, my back was numb, and my ankle stiff. After months of these conditions and monotony in the classroom, I was burning out. Teaching is not an easy job in our own country, let alone in a foreign one. I did my best to help the kids anyway I could. Sadly, many students did not want to learn. Thankfully Ivana and I had one more conference to attend that would break up the pattern.

We took the night train to Tbilisi. We waited on the cold platform for our tickets to be checked. We spent the night asleep, leaning on each other, our possessions in between us. I remember waking up to the occasional lurch in the warm car to look out onto the passing towns. The snow falling in the twilight, little sleeping villages, it was a beautiful moment from a midnight train in Georgia.

We arrived in daylight of the morning and I took Ivana to the Peace Corps' headquarters and showed her around. I let her go through the library and take whatever she wanted. I loaded up on some nice clothes from the free table. She met a few other volunteers who enjoyed talking with her. The other volunteers liked my counterpart and thought it was cute how close we were. Lisa met up with us and we went for pizza. Ivana was so ecstatic to be in Tbilisi and enjoying the volunteer life. She was more herself outside the village, she was no longer the good kept girl, she was Crazy Ivana. We took a taxi to the hotel. We grabbed our bags and found our rooms. It was Ivana and Anastasia in their room, and me and Lisa. Mjolnir was shacking up with his girlfriend, spreading peace that way. Make love, not war...they took that literally.

By evening we all met down in the dining hall for dinner. I saw her again, Anastasia, she came in wearing a black sweater, brown skirt, she smelled of vanilla. Lisa and Ivana walked in together, and we secured a table all to ourselves. The four of us were laughing like idiots all through dinner. I cracked a few risqué jokes that had both Ivana and Anastasia fall out of their seats. I was on fire that night, I guess she lit something in me.

Ivana was laughing so hard she could not breathe, "Why you make us laugh so much? She's a married woman. You want a married woman?"

Anastasia blushed as she looked away. "I like making people laugh," I said. I wanted her to laugh, and she did. This week would prove interesting. After the torrent of comedy subsided, we talked photography. Anastasia was a shutterbug like me and we tried to get the best photo of each other, we made a game of getting the most natural photo of each other. She won when she got a picture of me relaxing with a book. She was intelligent and beautiful, a deadly combination.

After dinner we went back to our rooms and grabbed our coats as we wanted to get photos by the Tbilisi Sea, and it was bitter cold. Lisa and I met them at the elevator where we started striking goofy poses. Outside the hotel, we walked in the blowing wind to the shore. I play fought with Ivana, she stole my hat from me, and we huddled together in the breeze. We did not care about anyone else but us four that night. It was our little group. Ivana loved Lisa and her jokes. Our own passionate group of innocent fun. By that point it was getting pretty late, and we were feeling tired from all the travel. We parted for the night. I took another hot bath and let the grime drift off of me. While I soaked, I drifted off to sleep in the warm water and awoke some half hour later only to dry off and crawl into bed.

I do not remember much of the day seminars. I did my round of looting, so did everyone else. Ivana and I sat side by side and cracked dumb jokes the whole time. For some reason all the male volunteers shaved their beards but kept the mustaches for a day. It did not look good. The only real thing I remember was this little seminar where everyone split into five groups. Four in each group and our job was to assemble cut out sentence fragments and make them into a story and tell us what it meant. It was me, Ivana, Mjolnir and his partner. I asked if I could take over and they agreed, we all thought it was dumb. I had it done in two minutes while everyone else had it done in ten while working together. It was a story of dogs running around separate and they came together to get food from this farm; it was a heart-warming story of cooperation. I was bored. I showed the rest of the group and they were bored too. I was in the right group. I asked if they minded if I changed it. They did not care. I reworked it and turned it into a horror story of how all the dogs came together to eat the outsider dog. Then presentation time came around. All the other groups went first and had the same story, then I presented my version. Several people look horrified. Lisa, Druggie, and those who enjoyed my company were nodding in agreement, stating they liked mine best. Mjolnir applauded, "That's a story."

After dinner, we went straight for the pool. It was a massive indoor pool and I had been swimming for a good thirty minutes when Ivana finally came down. She was with another Georgian teacher, a deeply, deeply intelligent woman. The basic demographic of all Georgian women, intelligent and beautiful. We swam together talking about life. Her story was tragic. While in her last year of high school she had become pregnant with her first daughter and was forced into marriage. Her mother raised the child while she finished her college education and started her career. She had regrets, she loved her child, but their relationship was that of sisters, not mother and daughter. Another marriage for social pressure. I heard this a thousand times, and always hated hearing about people trapped in horrible lives. You can drown in your own empathy if you do not learn how to swim in it.

I admired her, she was incredibly intelligent. On rare occasion, I find someone beyond normality, usually caused by societal trauma, that inspires me to shut the hell up in their presence, she was one. I still got her to laugh with a few laser-guided jokes, but I remained mostly silent, listening. I got the feeling she was not as close with her American as Ivana was with hers. Her husband, well she did not care, as I assume he did not either. A Georgian woman's life is nothing but a prison of regret.

Ivana talked about how English was overriding her thoughts and dreams to the point she thought only in English, and she had improved greatly. I colonized her mind. We talked about dreaming in other languages, a funny occurrence when you learn another language, you dream in it. The other teacher left the pool to call her daughter; Ivana and I were left to our own devices. We talked about our lives again, and wondering where the world would take us. She accused me of being a spy, I was not. It was a deep conversation we had as we glided through the water in tandem, occasionally joking about this or that. How much we had both changed in a short time. How we had both impacted each other. We loved each other as friends.

Then she came down. She walked out with a towel wrapped around her; she was blushing as I looked at her. She took a deep breath then opened her towel towards me. She was wearing a semi-conservative two-piece bikini, aqua-marine, and brand new. I swam in my own faded Hawaiian trunks which had seen better days. Her suit was spotless. I think this was the first time she ever wore a bikini in her life, her face was bright red whenever our eyes met. Ivana commented on how beautiful she was and shapely. All three of us swam closely together and spoke so only we could hear. While she was in the pool, she kept the water at neck level to cover herself. We occasionally did summersaults and spins in the water. The conversation was really lackluster, both of our thoughts were focused on other topics than the conversation at hand. We swam for a good hour before we decided to head back to their hotel room.

After dressing and showering, I found them in their hotel room. They were rebelling, smoking out the window. There is nothing more dangerous than a Georgian woman when she rebels. They had lived so long with their lives controlled by husbands, fathers, and men that they wanted to be their own women. Ivana invited me to sit, so I did. They sat right beside me on each side. The room was incredibly warm and I could smell everyone. I remember feeling dizzy from it all, pheromones like mustard gas, we all felt that. We joked and flirted coyly. Ivana asked the question.

Ivana, "If you weren't married, would you sleep with him?"

Anastasia turning bright red, "Would you?"

Ivana, "Well obviously."

Anastasia admits, "Yes."

All I had to do was reach out. As I sat there and looked into Anastasia's eyes, she looked back, but she was in pain, they both were. I could read it in their eyes and lives alike. She married because she was expected to, and realized she did not love her husband at all. He did not love her, he enjoyed her beauty, as any man would. She told me this. How much was she trying to escape her life? That young woman who had been locked away for years in a loveless marriage. My thoughts weighed heavily upon me.

I had to turn away from reaching out. I had to stop the procedure of events from taking place. It would be a temporary passion, but years of pain for both of us. I sat back. I could not do it. I would not harm her or her family. They were both trapped women. I stood up to open the door and aired out the room, I was choking under it all. That moment of character passed, and so with it the temptation. I told them both they were good women, and the most beautiful on Earth and deserved better than what life had handed them. I told them I had something to do. I left.

The next day the conference ended and Anastasia snapped another photo of me being natural. She was intelligent, and we said goodbye. I helped Ivana onto the train home as I decided to spend a few days with volunteers in Tbilisi. Due to every volunteer being present, all the hostels were full. I found one hostel for all six of us, my contribution at a moment's notice. I always helped fellow volunteers when I could. I ended up catching the train home to the village during a blizzard. I was on the train home when the emergency text from the Peace Corps reached me, telling us to avoid Batumi due to weather conditions. The Peace Corps staff were notified by a volunteer about the weather conditions, which prompted them to act late in the day. I was already on the train. The Peace Corps is not proactive, they are reactionaries. I ignored it and carried on without any problems.

As I pondered the events of the past week, I noticed a group of Iranian tourists on holiday trying to snap a group selfie. The Iranian man in the seat in front of me had lined up the photo so that his friends in his row and his friends beside me were lined up in a way that caused me to be caught in the photo as well. I could not go anywhere, so I smiled. It was funny, I was forced to be a photobomber by Iranians on holiday. He snapped the photo and it was honestly a nice one of all of us. It was a genuine smile. He turned and laughed after looking at it, "Good one." We got to chatting as we had hours together. He and his friends were on holiday.

We talked about our cultures and I apologized as an American for screwing over their country since Mossadegh. Politics aside, neither of us were in our own countries and were merely guests on a train. We spoke freely. Turns out people are the same everywhere you go, with some minor differences. They were relieved to find me a goofball American. They gave me one of the biggest compliments of my life: "You are not like the other Americans; you don't fear different cultures."

I thought about it for a moment, "I don't suppose I do. I look at it as if everyone has a piece of a puzzle. I have the American piece; you have the Iranian piece. I want to know what your world is like. It's like changing the channel or trying a different wine, only a little more complex." I really don't care about politics; politics is dumb everywhere. Pity others do not see it that way. I shared bottles of water and tea with them, they thanked me. They laughed when they saw my brick phone and asked how I got around. I showed them a paper map. The man laughed; he had not seen a paper map in years. Here I was, the backward American, "I prefer the old ways sometimes, best not to forget." He nodded.

HAMMERED TIME

After a couple more weeks of school, Maria had her wedding. I was the guest of honor. It was odd, Georgians are not wealthy, but they spend vast fortunes on their weddings. I showed up wearing my nice clothing, brandishing a decorated gift in silver wrapping paper. No one knew what it was. I was seated at the cousins table with her brother. The Tamada, the master of ceremonies, stood up and gave a beautiful toast. I understood half of it. Eventually the master of ceremonies dragged me to the microphone.

    I was the guest of honor and they asked me to give a special blessing from America. They brought her cousin in as a translator. I said the only blessing I knew which was an Irish one. I handed Maria her gift. I slipped them a hundred as well. She opened the gift and started laughing. She turned to show it to her husband, who started laughing as well. She held it up for the crowd to see, it was a hammer. The room erupted in laughter. I told her it was to keep him in line. She thanked me genuinely. My toast went over well. Her cousins, who worked as models, took an interest in me and spent the night dancing with me. We enjoyed the evening. I loved her family, and apparently, they loved me as many of them drunkenly told me. It was the best wedding I went to.

    Around four in the morning, the wedding wound down. On the ride home, her brother grabbed me by the back of the head and pulled my forehead to his, "You are goodman, know you are part of my family, you are my brother now, you are Georgian." We hugged each other. I got home by six, and fell asleep for two hours before my alarm went off for school. Ivana wanted me there to find worksheets and print off activities for projects she had in mind, something I could do while recuperating from a Georgian wedding. I was not supposed to teach, everyone understood I was at my first Georgian wedding.

I walked into the classroom, and to my shock and horror, a Georgian Project Manager from the Peace Corps was sitting there waiting to see how I taught class. The appropriate thing to do would have been to walk up and shake her hand and proceed with the lesson. Instead, I burst out laughing as I had just walked in from partying all night. I was screwed and I knew it, but in that situation all I could do was laugh. I was not supposed to teach as Ivana and I had planned ahead of time. Luckily, Ivana was friends with the Project Manager as they had a long history together, and she explained I was at my first wedding. The Manager was frustrated, "Did you not get my email, I sent it last week?"

I shook my head, "I haven't gotten a chance to see my email in over a week. We're in a dead zone here, no internet in or out. I can only see my email when I travel to the next town over." She sighed, this was supposed to be a yearly observation, but no one knew she was coming thanks to the technical difficulties of the environment. She rubber-stamped me, saying I had successfully culturally integrated. I was hungover. The only thing that matters is if the people like you, and they did. I sat behind the computer and printed off papers and answered pronunciation questions. Ivana and I were laughing; I am thankful they were goods friends. They were the type of friends that sent dirty jokes about dildos to each other. I saw the pictures they sent in private, downright dirty jokes.

ICE TO MEET YOU

The days droned on; my health got worse. The relentless march of homework, tests, quizzes, and grammar exhausted me. I was burning out. It seemed like all I did was relentlessly work until some medical problem sent me to the capital. I was constantly in physical pain, reported, and they did nothing to fix the problem. The only vacation I had during my service was when a group of volunteers wanted to go skiing in my region for a weekend. Thanks to my surgically reconstructed knee, all I could do was walk around on top of a mountain while everyone else skied. Not much of a vacation unless I wanted to risk breaking my knee, and risk my service. I took some good photos though. I had to make the best of it.

Sometime in march, during winter, we had a warm snap and it felt like late spring. I needed to break the monotony. I slapped on my swim trunks, and thought about the weather. At midday, if I stayed in the sun, I could dry off and warm up quickly. I walked to the waterfall, and into the pool at the bottom. This was mountain water, flowing down from where it was still frozen. I waded into the shallows, and jumped in. Immediately my body went into shock. It felt like I had been stabbed a hundred thousand times with needles all over my body. It was the coldest experience I ever had. My body contracted into a ball due to the sudden shock. I forced myself to swim across to the other side of the pool, about five meters. I had to consciously force each arm forward through the bone-chilling water.

The only way I could stay alive was by moving as fast as I could and ignore the cold. I pushed on, and made it to the other side and then back. It felt like my chest was being squeezed like a lemon in some satanic lemonade. Every part of my body pulled inward and I had to force my arms forward to move, all they wanted to do was curl up against my body. It was like swimming became rock climbing; I had to force my arms out to pull myself forward. It was the slowest and most difficult swim of my life. It was so cold, it felt like someone was dragging razors across my skin. I finally clamored back to where I jumped in, completing the lap. I was not in any danger, all I had to do was stand up as it was not that deep. I was only in the water thirty seconds.

My body was bright purple, all the blood flushed against my flesh. I looked like I was inside out. I grabbed my towel and dried off in the sun as fast as I could. Once in the sun, I was warm and no longer in danger of freezing to death. A horrible experience, yet I am a glad to know how to deal with freezing water. It was a controlled ice burn. I was getting my body use to extreme environments, in case a marshrutka went into the river in winter. In case of emergency, I bought myself a few more seconds. I walked back from the waterfall, several of the villagers were horrified to see me in swim trunks. It woke me out of the monotony. There were no lingering physical problems from this. I was not sick till a month later with my monthly strep throat.

PROJECTS

I was worked on many projects, trying to do the best I could for the children of Georgia, despite everything. There are many volunteers like this, my friends were all the same way, filling their time to do as much as possible in two years. At the same time, I was studying Georgian and trying to learn the language. I did not like my teacher, which hampered my efforts, but there were no real choices in the village. I was one of the few to continue studying Georgian; most Americans consider it a useless language.

I administered tests for my regional project, graded papers, and judged presentations for competitions. I fixed bicycles for another volunteer's project, led after school classes, volunteered for camps, and hosted events for libraries. I edited academic papers for professors at the university in Batumi. I even tutored a priest in English for a short time. I worked over forty hours a week. Anything I could do, I did, all free of charge.

My first big project was the regional spelling bee competition that I was the head of in Adjara. I had to oversee fifty different schools, train teachers, host events, direct local competitions, grade tests, and organize the regional competition involving a hundred students from all over the region. Then I had to pass everything on to the national competition. I spent months working, organizing, and committing myself to hundreds of administrative tasks. If any teachers had questions, I was the point of contact and had to make sure everyone knew what to do. We held the regional competition in Winter. Then we had to narrow a hundred students down to four. That was the hard part, and seeing students crushed made me hate spelling bees. They were all good kids who worked really hard.

After I turned in the required paper work, there was still a mountain of personal information I had to shred. I used the Peace Corps shredder at HQ. I asked first and was told it was fine. I was still questioned on it by another administrator who looked at me suspiciously, like I was doing something illegal. If I didn't ask, it would have been misuse of government property. I could have been terminated for that. I told her to go check with the person I asked, and she did. I am was happy I asked first. I followed the written rules.

The time came for the national spelling bee in Tbilisi, where I did not have to manage anything. I went to help out and support my region. I had a medical exam in Tbilisi at the same time, which all medical travel is paid for. I found out I was one of the most honest of the volunteers. All volunteers were to be reimbursed for travel for the spelling bee, about ten dollars for each way. I explained that I had come on medical travel and therefore would not take the reimbursement for travel from the spelling bee as I had not paid any of my own money. The Peace Corps Volunteer in charge of nationals looked at me shocked, "You're the only volunteer I have met who would stick to their morals and say no to money." She was a devout catholic and looked at me horrified. She was one of the die-hard volunteers who sat on several projects and committees. She was catholic like me, and as I knew her, thought she was a decent person. I guess if you are the most honest person in the Peace Corps, you have reached the end game, now what? I thought she was honest as me too, until then.

I did not take the money as the NGO needed it more for the students than myself. I thought that would be defrauding and stealing money from an NGO. I was not going to change out my morals for ten dollars. That is who I am. I felt alone after that conversation. I mean I could have signed the paper, lied, gotten ten dollars and walked away with no repercussions. I said no, I only had myself to answer to. Every Peace Corps

Volunteer I spoke to about this told me I should have taken the money, including a current day investigator for the US government. Even my friends, devout Catholics, all of them told me I should have lied and taken the money. How much they all told me I should have lied bothered me a lot. Their rationalizing was that we were there to work, and we were not paid, anything to help us helps the project. Even Ms. Lisa took money she was not supposed to, small change to cover costs for projects, which still went against the rules. I felt alone, was I the only one following the rules? In the Peace Corps, a small amount of corruption is expected, altruists are the freaks. This is one of those moments where I saw the rest of the group, I considered these people good, but they were all telling me I should have lied. I would have felt relentlessly guilty about the whole thing and it would have eaten me alive more than the food I was eating. This bothered me. I was isolated by my own honesty in the Peace Corps.

I felt like an imposter. The more I thought about it, the worse I felt for doing the right thing. Here I was doing everything to make the world better. It made no sense to me. Would everyone else take ten dollars without regard to morality? All the volunteers I asked, told me I should have taken the money, but that would have been fraud. I no longer felt comfortable. It was an unsettling realization. I found out some other Peace Corps Volunteers were supplementing their stipend by tutoring off the books, which is not allowed, but once again the Peace Corps turns the other way as long as their image is not threatened. I held myself to super high standards, and I did not even realize it. What did it get me? I was losing everything, my health, living in pain, living on less than ten dollars a day. Was this worth it? What had my morals bought me? For all the good I was doing, in the end, all I was told was that my digestive tract was being eroded and I was risking cancer, and I should have lied. I was being eaten alive every day. The doctors did nothing to address it. The pain carried on, and so did I. I was overworking and underfed to the point I was back to my high school weight when I was fifteen.

ABSOLUTE FUTILITY

Throughout the year I had been developing my government funded project, the crowning jewel of my achievements in the Peace Corps, building a small library. This involved budgeting, grant writing, and all the wonderful paperwork behind a government funded project. It was something that would be a lasting investment for the community. At the beginning of the school year, Ivana had shown me what she wanted. There was an abandoned apartment that was boarded up and used for storage by the school. She wanted to turn it into a library where she could teach and hold after school programs where students could learn English. A place where students could rest and have a safe place to learn away from parents, school, smoking, and drinking. She wanted me to build a library. I could do it. There are programs in place through the Peace Corps where volunteers can propose and build projects to get funding, small projects under five thousand dollars. Enough to build a small library, which volunteers have done.

For months I worked, analyzing, budgeting, finding community members who would work for free, where I could get books, shelves, couches, cabinets, computers, and everything for a small library. Ivana found people who were willing to renovate this old abandon apartment, and turn it into a cozy little library and after school program. Infrastructure is not allowed in Peace Corps grants, so we had to find people willing to do the labor for free and who had extra material they would be willing to donate. My counterpart knew where to go for the materials and workers. I spent the school year working on this, talking with grant writers, villagers, the school, and budgeting. All to fulfill a dream my partner teacher wanted for our students. I emailed dozens of companies and donors who could donate books. I had everything figured out and I started preparing for the grant application. We even received a plethora of books which we opened with delight. The principal thanked me for my work and contribution.

Then it happened. One weekend while I was sick again, strep throat, I noticed villagers clearing out the old abandoned apartment near the school. I happened to look out the window and saw students moving debris. I thought, oh how odd they are clearing it early. Then it struck me, "No!" I dressed and ran down with my fever. One of the teachers at the school up and decided to take the apartment for herself. The property laws are different in villages in different countries and she claimed it as being abandoned property. No one was willing to intervene. I called Ivana who called the principal who called the super intendant who eventually called me saying there was nothing they could do. The principal and the super intendent were from other villages and did not want to involve themselves in the affairs of a different village. Call it village politics. Months of my hard work wasted, Ivana's dreams crushed, my own aspirations ruined.

The teacher who took the apartment knew about the project. At the beginning of the year, the principal made an announcement that I would be turning the apartment into a library. She crushed the project, saying she needed it more than the village. Then she called me a tourist, saying I did not care about Georgia. Volunteers will find people like this all around the world, willing to steal from their own village's children. My motivation and morale took a huge hit after that. I could not muster any motivation to start any new projects. I learned the villagers did not care about my work or what I was sacrificing. I was just an English teacher in their eyes, a tourist, nothing more. Volunteers come and go, and that is what a Peace Corps Volunteer is, someone who comes to leave. To the locals, a volunteer is a glorified tourist.

Never forget, a volunteer could sacrifice everything and the locals do not care. All my motivation slunk out of me. I started wearing blue jeans to school instead of black slacks. Months of work for nothing. I had to carry on though, I could not waste time whining about my project despite it being destroyed. I had to adapt, improvise, and overcome. I funneled what motivation I had left into helping the kids learn so they did not stay in the village. I was doing two after school programs a week. I carried on. Nothing destroys motivation like learning how the people you came to help, do not care. A reality of the Peace Corps, those you came to help do not care.

STANDARDIZED TESTING

For the seniors to graduate, they had to pass a final exam. Ivana told me to come to the school at a different time than usual, as she said the students, "needed help with their exams". They did not tell me what was going on.

The students asked her in Georgian, "How is he going to help? He hates cheating on tests."

She calmed them down, "He will help, I know him."

Nothing sums up Georgian mentality like what I saw that day. The test was on a single computer, set up with a camera to watch the student and the room. The camera did not have a microphone. I showed up and immediately saw the operation. The teachers had a station set up in the hallway with a camera and a long-range lens on a tripod, aimed at the computer screen. The students took the photo, read the question, the respective teacher solved the problem, and then yelled the answer to the student sitting at the computer. It was an operation. The seniors watched me hesitantly, not sure of what I would say or do. Their lives depended on these exams to graduate high school.

I sat down beside Ivana and read the English questions, and gave the answers while a student yelled out the corresponding letters. I sat there for a long time as each individual student went in. Finally, the last student went in, a girl who spoke a little English. She was a good kid, smart, but no one ever invested in her learning, or her value as a person. Her own family expected her to pop out babies as soon as she graduated, nothing more. We got her through half of the answers when Ivana said, "she passed, were done." Ivana was willing to abandon her own student. I got angry at her for that. As much as a feminist as she claimed to be, she was willing to abandon her female students, doing the least for her.

I heard the student beg for help in English, "Help me!" She looked back at us worried.

I put my hand on Ivana's shoulder, "No one gets left behind. We're not abandoning her because she passed, let's get her at least a B+."

Ivana relented as the students were starting to pack up, abandoning their own. "Ok, fine." I yelled at the students to get back to their positions. They snapped to as I was using my loud voice like when I found a cheater in class and was about to tear up a test. We helped the student finish up. Once she was done, she sighed, thanking me. Ivana wanted to give her a passing D and did not care to give her a decent score. I shamed her on that for abandoning a young woman. "Fine, you win Mr. American." She knew I was right.

"Best sentence I've ever heard you say." I had all the students and Ivana come into the classroom for a post-operation debrief. "I'm sure you are all curious why I helped you all."

They all nodded. "Yes, you hate cheaters. Why now?" The smartest student asked in English, exasperated.

"The grades in class are for you to know where you are, they are for you to learn. That dumb test is for the government to decide your life. It is not for you at all. It is a controlling tool developed by a bureaucrat."

As Ivana translated, they lay back in their chairs as they understood.

I continued, "In class, you idiots cheat to get a good grade, not even bothering to ask why. In university, no one is going to help you in your exams. You will fail if you need to cheat for a grade." They understood, life is not about grades, it is about learning. School was revealed not to be a place of learning, but grades. I was prepping them for the next step in life. Lisa had taught me the most important lesson on the beach as she lay under the sun, "Don't let schooling ruin your education." I told this to them. I wanted them to succeed in life.

They passed their tests. They took me out to celebrate with them. We all went to the restaurant and had dinner and drinks that night. Even the trouble maker who set the trashcan on fire was toasting me. We drank to their graduation. That night was the first time I drank out of a shoe. They were no longer my students, they graduated. The girl Ivana abandoned got drunk and kept thanking me for supporting her, "I love America," she said drunkenly, "thank you". She asked, "Why did you help me?"

"You are a smart young woman, I believe in you, and you need to believe in yourself." She started crying and hugged me. I gave her a small hug back, "You need to go to university." She nodded and released me. I think I was the first person to ever acknowledge her as a thinking person. Her life was devoid of any support for who she was, no one ever listened to what she wanted. Her father, I never met him, but he expected and told her to get married and start having kids as soon as she was out of high school. This is common in the villages. What a hell.

The next day Ivana and I sat down with her, "You need to go to university, we will tutor you twice a week in English for free and prepare you for next year." We were both planning on teaching her for free, two on one, to get her prepped for university. Helping her gave me a renewed hope for my work in the Peace Corps. To get at least one student out of a horrible life would have made it all worthwhile. At this point in her life, she turned eighteen, graduated from high school, and the village and her father were all telling her to get married and have kids. I hated that. I told her as much, "Don't listen to your parents, they are setting you up for failure. Ask yourself, is your mother happy?"

Ivana translated. She stopped, thought, and shook her head. She was fighting herself internally, fighting her own family. Everyone was telling her to be like them, and here we were offering a chance for her to be herself. She agreed to it. She wanted to be better. Ivana and I made plans to tutor her twice a week for a year to get her ready for the next year's admissions test. The next day she stood up for herself and said no to the twenty-year-old idiot that was pressuring her to reproduce. Everyone was shocked that she wanted to go to university. I was proud of for her, she deserved better than to be breeding stock and a domestic slave. No one deserves that hellscape. I was happy for her, and I told her as much.

I had to work on a project for a nearby volunteer for a few days. By the time I returned, she was married. In one week, all plans were dashed. When she saw me next, she would not make eye contact. I only told her, "Go to university." I met with Ivana, "What happened while I was gone?"

"Her father made her change her mind." I feared that was the case. How Georgian men treat women is the worst thing about Georgia. All female volunteers say the same thing in Georgia, "I have never had so much respect for American men." This was my biggest failure in the Peace Corps. This was more crushing than my library project. The lost potential of a human life. There was not anything I could do. I had to move on. I did not have time to waste feeling sorry for her. Nine months later she became her family's hopes and dreams.

SUMMER TIME

The school year was over and I took a breath. I needed to take some time for myself. I had been hollowed out from everything I had been through. I needed a break. I cancelled my Georgian lessons with my Georgian teacher for the summer and planned to resume in fall. I was getting little from our lessons as it felt like she did not care. I have fun learning, but this felt like pulling teeth. You have to find a tutor you can connect with, and that can be difficult. I traveled around helping out at summer camps and other projects, teaching English and doing my volunteer work. I spent my free time at the restaurant studying Georgian with Aksana who studied Turkish. We sat together and joked, drinking coffee while we studied.

I had to think about everything that worked and did not work and gear up for my second year. The second year is where everyone finishes their projects. First thing I needed to figure out was the food problem. I contacted the Peace Corps manager in charge of the living arrangements to figure out some solution. My stomach problems were getting worse by the month and were causing constant pain.

The Peace Corps requires three houses for the application process for a site. They choose the one that looks the best and they have backups. Volunteers in Georgia have to live with a family, unless they can find another apartment or house within walking distance from their place of work. Unless the volunteers are willing to pay their own money, they have to live off the monthly stipend with no change in pay. In my village, there were no apartments. I called and the Peace Corps and explained my health problems and they said, "Just stay where you are." I asked about the backup arrangements. Their reply, "they wouldn't work."

"There are supposed to be three options for back up. You don't want me to request a new one?"

"You're in the best one."

It dawned on me. The three options were only on paper, and there was only one real choice. I was stuck. I was forced to deal with all the stresses of the Peace Corps while my insides were burning from the food I was forced to eat. My host father was not going to spend more on food, but he continued to gamble every week. I asked for more food, he gave me a cabbage. I asked again, he told me to eat raw fish. If I was having stomach problems, he told me to drink vodka. This is the Peace Corps, I was stuck risking cancer, the doctors did not care, nor did the administration, and the locals did not care either. No one cares in the Peace Corps.

"If you can find another place to live, you can move out on your own."

"There are no places for rent here, I'm in a village." I would not even be able to afford an apartment either. I was living on 250 dollars a month, and the cheapest apartment I ever heard about was three hundred dollars, and Georgians charge in dollars. I would not be able to afford food and I would have to spend my own money, which the Peace Corps says we should not. The Peace Corps is a master of double talk. The Peace Corps is designed for volunteers who are wealthy.

This is the mentality of the Peace Corps: if the volunteer has the money, then they can get their own place if they can find one, and the administration will turn a blind eye as long as the volunteer is not causing problems. The rule book says that volunteers "should not" spend their own money, but this rule is only enforced it the volunteer is causing problems. The Peace Corps only enforces the rules when the image of the Peace Corps is under scrutiny.

The Peace Corps, like everything else in America, it serves the wealthy first. This elitism has always been part of the Peace Corps. The Peace Corps was established in the 60's and was aimed at college kids, and back then, most of the college kids were from wealthier families as less than 10% of the adult population of America went to college at that time. A college degree is a requirement for the Peace Corps. That is the upper 10% of the US population, the wealthier families. The Peace Corps was created for several reasons: as a means to get college student votes for JFK, to improve the Foreign Service, and to counter Cold War communist propaganda. What better way to show poor countries that capitalism is a better choice over communism, than by having the children of the wealthy go out and help the children of poor countries. Communist propaganda at that time was focused on workers over-throwing greedy capitalists. Realpolitik is not allowed in the Peace Corps.

Today, the college educated population of America is closer to 40%. More volunteers are coming from lower-income families, but that image of the wealthy American volunteer helping the poor continues, it is called American Exceptionalism. If the volunteer does not have the money, then they are forced to live on a bare bones budget that can be hazardous to their health, like mine was. The Peace Corps cares about what is cheapest for the budget, not what is best for the volunteer. This treatment is reflected in the post-service medical care of the Peace Corps. The wealthier volunteers do not need any post-service medical support, because they can afford better healthcare and will likely have a government job after their service. The volunteers who need help are brushed under the rug and forced to deal with the Department of Labor, where a volunteer might be lucky enough to get surgery two years after the problem started. The "image" of the Peace Corps, is that of wealthy Americans going out and helping poor foreign children. Lower-income volunteers go against the Peace Corps image. The Peace Corps is for rich kids.

It is Hobson's Choice housing in the Peace Corps. In Georgia, you are forced to live with a family, but the Peace Corps tells you are free to move out, only there is nowhere to move to. Volunteers have to be within walking distance of their place of work. There was no choice available, they sent me there knowing there was no other place to live. That is the Peace Corps, as long as it looks good on paper. I was stuck, forced to spend more of my own tiny stipend on paying for food for which I was already paying.

Georgia is one of the few Peace Corps programs that does this. I have met volunteers who served in Africa and they showed me pictures of these spacious apartments, penthouses, beautiful homes they rented, and told me how affordable it was on their stipend. Other countries were also paid in dollars, not the local currency. In Georgia, we were paid in Lari, yet landlords in Georgia wanted rent in dollars. The Peace Corps told us we made enough money to live on, comparable to the level of the people we were serving. The only volunteers I have ever heard of living on their own in Georgia on their stipend, were a married couple who had twice the stipend for living. You are lucky if you can find an apartment for cheap, but that is extremely rare. The Peace Corps wants to keep it cheap to pay the volunteers the lowest they can, if it is too expensive, peace is not worth it. You volunteered for it and you have to respect the tax payer's dollar. I was told that by the administration of the Peace Corps. I was serving America for free and sacrificing my time and health. It didn't matter. Peace Corps, cheaper than the military. There is cheap, then there is Peace Corps cheap.

I was stuck with an already shrunken budget, needing medical help without any doctor helping me. The doctors said what damage was happening without any diagnosis or way to fix the problem. The Peace Corps only treats symptoms, they do not want to diagnose. If the doctors diagnose a problem, that means the US government is responsible for it, if they do not diagnose, then there is no problem they are responsible for. The Peace Corps does not want to take care of your health, it is not important. The Peace Corps is the cheapest organization in the US government, and I was serving for free. I dreamed of making the money a new recruit in the army made, and soldiers ate better and had far better medical care. The US government does not care about the volunteers, which means the work of the volunteers does not matter to the government. The image of the volunteer is more important than the volunteer.

The only thing I could think of was to tutor for food, at least that way I could get a hot meal once in a while. I worked for food, I felt like a beggar. Peace Corps Volunteer, will work for food. The other volunteers

I visited, many of them ate well and had many options, mine, potato. There were no real options in the Hobson's Choice Corps. The Peace Corps does this to show the locals we are just like them. This is an excuse to be cheap. Polyps were growing in my intestines and my digestive track was being eroded away.

I revaluated my projects. With many of them now completed or destroyed, I had to figure out a new strategy. I carried on tutoring as usual and started planning for additional projects for my last year. I tried to figure out my problems and carry on with my service. I still carried on with the mission. No one did anything to help me change my situation, and when I requested a change, I was told to, in the immortal words of our Peace Corps Country Director, "Suck it up." No one wanted to change anything, once you are in the Peace Corps, they want to leave you there for two years and ignore you. They did not care about my complaints, despite serving in pain, I still carried on. Once you are at your site, they don't care about you. I will never forget this.

A HAPPY MEMORY

I still carried on teaching, doing the most I could to help the kids and their families. I grew to see them as my own family. I am a family man, and helping those kids meant the most to me, I guess that is why I kept going. I loved Georgia, Sakartvelo, and America, and I kept working despite it all. Every week I went and tutored my second-grade student, now a third grader. I went in the evenings and tutored English with her and her sister. Her parents were happy to have free lessons. That girl was a language sponge, she memorized everything. She copied my intonation, syntax, everything and used it perfectly when speaking in seconds flat. My second-grade student was the smartest person I ever met. A seven-year-old girl was smarter than any Harvard trained professor at my university, and better than any diplomat with languages. This was a humbling moment in my life. I found out she was Ivana's niece. Everyone is related in the village.

That is why I am writing this. The Peace Corps needs to change, but there are still people who need help. I know I get angry about my experience, as any rational human would, but I am doing this to improve conditions for the volunteers. The Peace Corps serves a purpose, which unfortunately is spreading American Exceptionalism and training personnel for the Foreign Service. It needs to change and get away from its

Cold War counter-propaganda origins and be what it claims to be, and not this two-faced bureaucracy.

I helped my student's family make traditional foods, an unmasculine thing, but as a foreigner I could get away with it and take the recipes back to share with family and friends. That idea everyone liked. I took part in making *tremali*, a special sauce, and I sat with the mothers cleaning berries. I listened to them speak. I felt at home here, like I was listening to my grandmother talk. I was home. Later in the evening I had to help bring in the cows. I befriended one. I sat there and scratched behind its horn and treated it like a dog, its eyes widened and it started nuzzling me. It started following me around. Everyone laughed as I stood there petting the cow saying in Georgian, "Who's a good cow? Vin aris gargi dzroha?" There I was, this odd American petting a cow in the mountains of Adjara.

This was the moment I remember, where I used the word home, and I understood what that meant. I felt like I belonged. Even the family who owned the restaurant welcomed me warmly every time with a cup of tea. I helped bust tables and clean every night, and tutored their kids. My nihilist sailor friend even asked me to stand guard when drunk tourists were harassing the girls who worked there. I stood with them. Some volunteers will pour their heart and soul into their work, I know I did. These were the last good memories I had, as all my housing and food problems would be solved.

WATER TEMPLE

This is how I almost became a Peace Corpse Volunteer. At this time, another volunteer in my region had been sexually assaulted and moved to a different location. Violence against volunteers is common, far more than what the Peace Corps reports. It was a normal day. It is always a normal day. A summer day, hot, and the water was inviting. I spent the day on the beach reading, talking with my students, trying to relax while my insides rotted and burnt out. One of the high school students stole my sunglasses from my face and ran off with them. I smiled and let her run away with them. I saw Maria's brother up the river and decided to go for a swim.

I waded out into the river as always, and started swimming upstream. The river was deep in some places, and in the middle of the river, if you swam at a steady pace going upriver, you went nowhere. I was pushing hard upstream; I swam to the second bend in the river where the current did not move as fast. Some of my high school students were there. The one who loved talking music with me, whose father was hard on him, was there. There was a second kid with anger issues who hit girls in class, and a third kid who sat there on the rocks. By the time I swam by, I was already out of breath fighting the current.

Something happened in my mind, like a red alert siren going off, it was the way the kid with anger issues was looking at me. I was in the middle of the river, treading. My students came out to meet me, coming off the rocks a few meters away. The kid with the anger issues swam behind me. I joked with the student who was always hanging around me, we splashed each other as a greeting in summer fun. The student with anger issues was behind me, fully in my blind spot and getting closer. The hairs on my neck rose. I tried to swim away to put distance between us when he jumped me. His hands pushed down on my head and I was forced under for a few seconds before I bobbed into the air again, enough time to spit the water out of my mouth before his hands grabbed my head. He gripped my skull this time. My arms and legs pushed hard against the force keeping my head submerged. I tried swimming in different directions, I could not move. I sank, and was forced down. I struggled hard, I tried grabbing the hands on my head but they had a firm grip on my skull, I sank even farther. The water was cold in the shadow. As I struggled, I thought I was being dunked as a prank, and usually the joke only lasts a few seconds. As I struggled, I thought, "ok, any second, I will be brought back up and be able to breathe" as I tried to climb to the surface and break the hold on my head.

Time stretched on; my air ran out. I screamed under water, a muffled empty airless scream. I remained struggling trying to push myself up into the air, the thing I wanted more than anything else. Air to breathe, what drowning men desire most. I was living in a sheer moment of terror. I do not know how long I was under; it was an absurdly long time as I had time to think. I can remember trying different tactics to free myself, thinking, and losing time. My lungs started to burn, it felt like my chest was going to explode. My throat opened on its own and tried to breathe. I ended up trying to swallow the river to clear my throat. It must have been some reflex as I tried to swallow the river. My throat hurt, but that pain seemed to not matter. I felt sick to my stomach as I chugged mouthfuls in a second. I could not breathe and my lungs wanted to open on their own and fill with water, they did not care, they wanted to open. I had to force my throat to slam shut. I thought, "no matter what happens, I can't let water in my lungs." I choked myself by forcing my throat closed. My lungs were burning like they were on fire, it felt like my ribs were too tight in my chest. Every thought in my mind was forced on making sure I asphyxiated to death before I drowned, that way I could live a few seconds longer. Every single thought was forced on killing myself before I drowned at his hands. My body was screaming to let me breathe, tempting me to open up and let the water in. To give in and breathe was the most tempting thing in my life. I refused. If the water went in my lungs at all, there would be no coming back. That was the final temptation, the siren's call, let go and breathe the water, ease the pain in my chest, end the inferno in my lungs, let the water end the burning, to let go and find peace. I found out who I was that day. Peace is a fatal lie; I would rather fight to the death than give in. I burned the temptation from my mind and tightened whatever muscle was in my throat. I say how and when.

I had my eyes open and watched the world as I was leaving it. It was odd, I usually saw air bubbles come out of my mouth and over my face when underwater. There was nothing, there was nothing leaving my body. The sounds I could hear were only a mix of gargling and the sound of choking as I was killing myself to stay alive. It was like that scene from *Star Wars*, when the force was revealed, choking a man. The sound reminded me of my favorite childhood movie. That choking noise. It sounded like that, except inside my head. Time stretched out, I had to hold on for as long as possible. I do not know how long I was under, it felt like forever. The world slowed further once I realized I was going to die. I stopped moving and sank despite kicking my legs, still choking myself.

The world became still and I could not feel anything anymore. The moment of screaming terror turned into an eerie peace. The chocking sound seemed distant. I looked up as much as my pinned head could and saw the light. I am not talking about God. When I was under the waves, I saw the sun through the water. The edges of my vision were dark, turning black, the water itself turned an odd turquoise color, and when I looked up, the world stopped. I looked up and saw the golden white gold halo of the sun and the closer I looked to the center, the whiter it blinded while the edges became brilliantly golden. Before, my frantic vision darted round and round looking for any way out. I became still and focused on the light, an encompassing warmth. The pain in my lungs and throat faded away. I could no longer feel my limbs, the exhaustion and horror left me at once. It was as if I was a head stuck in time peering into the most beautiful light of my life, nothing could ever come close to how beautiful that light was, gold on the edges, a pure white in the center. I no longer cared about the past, present, or future, there was no time, I just was.

I do not know what made it so beautiful, disassociation, lack of oxygen to the brain, or whatever. I remember the sheer terror that it was the end, and seeing the beautiful light and thinking: "Oh, how pretty." That was the last thought I had to the last thing I saw; I was preparing to die in a real and horrifying manner. When drowning, you watch yourself die. Nothing mattered to me then, peace, conflict, America, only the beauty of existence. Perhaps I should consider myself lucky to see the reality of the world, and to live. I realized the truth later. The light I was looking at was the mountain with its granite top reflecting the light of the sun down on me, the sun was behind me, behind the teenager trying to kill me, and what I saw was only the reflection of the light. So beautiful and golden, so beautiful in time. It eclipsed the fear of the end, I overcame fear. The most beautiful thing I ever saw in my life was when I was drowning for America. The moment stretched on, and I was happy to remain forever there, it was so beautiful while the world around so vividly mortifying.

That light was so unearthly beautiful. I have lived and came close to death, and have seen the enrapturing terror. How much I found truth in my life in the moment, where all realities are removed saved one, I am alive. The Peace Corps will persecute me after everything I went through for them, and I lost everything for the them. I sacrificed more than the vast majority, yet they will come after me to defend their prized image and their salaries. I lost everything in service to the country that threatened me after I almost gave my life for them. The Peace Corps is pathetic to threaten a victim. I am alive and I have come to love the terror of what it means to exist. I survived, and that is all that matters. How free in my dying light I became.

The pressure was gone, the hands were gone. I realized I could move my neck. Terror flooded my mind; I was now fully aware. "MOVE!" That was the thought I had, as a sudden purpose filled my mind as fear of tomorrow crept back into my existence. The beautiful moment disappeared in the blink of an eye and reality arose once more. I felt my body flood with adrenaline; everything my body had after millions of years of evolution, dumped everything it had to keep me alive. It worked, the body survived after being broken and broken repeatedly. I came back once more. I flung my hands above me, as I did the breast stroke 1.5 cycles. I say one and a half because after I completed one full cycle with my arms fully extended, half way through the second I breached the surface. I was rising so fast I felt like a rocket and flung my body out of the water. As soon as my nose hit air, I spewed out the water trapped in my airway and gulped in the atmosphere. It felt as if I could never breathe enough and that my lungs were exploding at the sudden inflation. I was never so happy to breathe. Once I hit the surface, I realized the full extent of my bodily exhaustion as I suddenly lost muscle control and started to sink once again, so exhausted I could barely move.

I saw the student who liked me, *The Kinks* student, and reached out to him as I started to go under again. He grabbed my hand as I sank back under the water, he pulled me to the rocks. I climbed up onto them. Jagged, they bruised and stuck me in odd angles as I lay on top of them, but it was as soft and welcoming as a pillow. Breathing rapidly, I stabilized my breath, I leaned over letting all water pour out of me. I felt high on air as my body took in the vital ether. I lay there face down on the rocks, feeling numb, my thoughts having trouble organizing, I was in shock. I can remember the two thoughts most of all racing through my head, "Take it easy, calm down and breathe, just breathe." The other, "Locate the threat." I followed the former for about ten minutes. My body was in shock, my mind reeling as I looked down on the rocks. Time moved on. I was vaguely aware of the other beings around me. The others had faces of uncertainty, they kept their distance. Only my music loving student did not fear, what did he have to fear?

Once I had enough oxygen, my peripherals started tracking the student that tried to kill me, to know his location was now priority. I used to wonder if his goal was to kill me or to prank me. The only thing I know is I was under so long, I went into shock, and had no bubbles coming out, and I was still as the grave when I saw the light, not even treading water, and my violent thrashing turned limp. Only then did his hand move from my head, he might have been trying to kill me and once he thought I was dead did he stop, especially if he was going through one of his rage issues. One thing was certain, for how deep I was, as judged by my swimming up to the surface, he had to be extending his arms and putting his full weight on my head to keep me under. When I stopped trying to swim up, he had to sink with me. He would have been forced to let go as I had been the only thing keeping him up. I was more than a meter underwater, as judged by my extended arms. To keep his own head above water, he had to let go. My being frozen in the light saved my life.

Only the student who grabbed my hand did not fear, he helped me when I reached out. I would later give him a quarter, something he did not have for his collection of international coins. He was so happy to have a dumb twenty-five cent piece, the worth of saving my human life. I laugh at this story; I should have given him a dollar. You know, perhaps I am as cheap as the Peace Corps. I should have given him a dollar.

After resting on the rocks to regain my strength, I called the student who tried to kill me a "son of a dog," which in their language means something offensive. I coiled my knees and launched myself back into the river. I dived for the fastest part of the current which carried me back down to the beach with minimal effort. I aimed myself at the sandy shore like a missile.

I heard it said you can never enter the same river twice; no man leaves the river the same as he entered. A different man crawled out of the river that day, and he collapsed on the sandy banks. I had put up with harassment from cops, my guts rotting, potatoes, freezing, working an exhausting number of hours every day, marching through the ice and snow to help these people, it cost me everything and for what? For the Peace Corps, I had suffered so much to my body, and being as friendly and dedicated as possible. That day I almost died for America, and what good did it do me? What good did being a helping person get me, nearly killed in the Peace Corps by the people I came to help. I watched myself be victimized and draw closer to death by the millisecond. It was a memory that forever changed me. I used to sit idly by while being insulted by other Peace Corps Volunteers. My guts were rotting on the food I survived on, being as goodwilled as possible and to make America look as good as possible. I collapsed on the beach, but the voice in the back of my head was screaming to get moving. I rinsed the sand off me and went back to my hovel of a room.

I broke down when I was alone. All the fear that had been bottled up in the seconds closest to death suddenly burst out when I was alone. In my vision, the world twisted in on me, I had trouble breathing, and I was so cold, yet it was summer. I was colder than in the winter. I never experienced that before, the weird psychological cold. I did not know what was happening to me. I called Doctor Vrach to advise me on what to do. I trusted her. She asked if I wanted to come to the capital for a week to rest. I remember saying no, I was trying to manage the situation without having to waste taxpayer money. That is what I said. I paid more in taxes than the billionaire president and here I was serving America for free and trying to not waste a hundred dollars. I was afraid of being kicked out on psychological grounds, as the Peace Corps threatens to kick out people for any psychological reason. The Peace Corps does not want to deal with psychological problems. The volunteers are there to help countries, but the volunteers are too afraid to ask for help themselves, as they will be punished for asking. No psychological help was offered.

What a Peace Corps fanatic I had become. I listened to the Peace Corps administration like I listened to my professors, only the professors were there to teach, the Peace Corps is there to manipulate. I should have taken the break, but I had work to do, tutoring to do, and other projects. Instead of taking time for myself, I carried on, still believing in the mission, I carried on for Georgia and America.

Doctor Vrach told had me speak to the Security Manager to report the incident. She asked if I wanted to press charges, I said no, not to ruin some dumb high schooler for life and cause an international incident. I was still under the belief he was joking, thinking of the good in everyone. I was is drowning. Only later would I piece together that he was trying to kill me. I thought about what his family had, they had nothing, they were poor. Perhaps I am too good of a man. I did my best to carry on. I had to report it, I called the Peace Corps to advise on the situation, and I had no idea what to do about this, as there is nothing in the rule book about situations like this. I can remember the Security Manager's words, "We will put the fear of God into him." I did not know what that meant and I was left confused after the phone call.

"What did that mean?"

I was so physically exhausted I blacked out. I remember waking up tense; I did not recognize my surroundings. I walked down to the river early in the morning and when I looked at it, my head involuntarily turned away. When I forced myself to look, my vision distorted and I broke down crying. It was as painful as looking into the eclipse. The one thing I loved more than anything else, swimming, was being taken away from me. I refused, I was done playing games with people, including myself.

I dived back into the river and started swimming. My mind was screaming at me to get out. I was terrified to be in the water, terrified to drown, to regain the thing I loved, water and swimming. It felt like ice when I jumped in, the physical manifestation was terrifying, it was not even like water but more of a foggy scary haze as my vision twisted as I swam. Every stroke felt like I was swimming through cement. I swam over the spot I almost drowned in, retaking everything for myself. No more will be taken from me, I thought. They had taken everything else, but the water is mine.

As I walked out of the river this time, I was breathing hard, but it was a fierce determination to stay alive no matter what. I was still on edge after almost being killed by the people I came to help, I knew I had to relax and heal, I had a job to do. After the river, I headed to town to be with other volunteers, I needed to be around Americans, I needed support. My hands kept clenching uncontrollably. If I took a drink of something, if I was not paying attention, I would start to cough and choke to clear my airway. Subconsciously I was still fighting to keep water out of my lungs. I was afraid of the Peace Corps administration to seek psychological help, as that is what the system is designed to do. It is designed to make you not seek help.

COMPASSION

I arrived and went to a little restaurant to meet my 'friends', we sat around talking. I told them about the previous day, they seemed to ignore it. I can remember sitting there zoning out, trying to rest and process everything. I was still in shock. Almost drowned to death by the people I came to help. I sat there around American volunteers, my fingers kept flexing into a fist.

Almost being killed in service to your country comes into perspective when it is your life on the line. The Peace Corps does their best to downplay the negative sides of serving. There are many dead Peace Corps Volunteers, and even one killed by Peace Corps doctors. Kate Puzey was murdered for reporting child molestation to the Peace Corps. For serving world Peace and trying to protect children in Africa, she was murdered. Reporting anything in the Peace Corps is tantamount to suicide, no one will protect you. The murderer walked away free after his fellow countrymen acquitted him, a child molester. When in international situations, the foreign country will always protect its own over foreign victims. They do it to save face, as it is better to protect a murderer over admitting your country has one. America and the Peace Corps are no different, they protected the murderer of Deborah Gardner. Lisa's words haunted me, "We're here for propaganda." I was trying to calm myself and heal from the previous day's trauma with other Americans.

At this time, we had a new volunteer in the area. This volunteer had been rude and insulting since day one and never stopped, passive aggressive and insulting, a toxic personality. This volunteer came late to the group at the restaurant, the rest of us, four or five volunteers were sitting there. As I sat there trying to process my own near-death and carry on for the mission, this Volunteer came to the restaurant and yelled at me, just came in and yelled, "Move your bag!" I was processing the trauma, still in shock. My bag was right beside me, leaning against my leg.

Next thing I know, this Volunteer yelled at me, lifted a chair up, and slammed it down right on top of my bad knee. The knee that had been operated on when I was a child to allow me to walk, a knee that cost thirty thousand dollars to fix. The Volunteer put their weight into it, the chair slid down my leg, scraping down the front of my leg and slammed onto my foot, crushing my backpack, as my bag was leaning against my leg. The volunteer was attacking me for a spot at the table, not even saying excuse me like a normal person. Instead, she chose to hit me with a chair and crush my possessions. Then the volunteer walked around the chair and sat down on it.

"What are you doing?"

"I wasn't aiming for your leg." Then the Volunteer smiled and ordered a beer.

"Learn some respect."

I went to the local computer and wrote up a report and filed it for harassment against another volunteer for the Security Manager. When you are in your country of service, you are on the job 24/7 even while you sleep, and the entire country is your workplace, it is workplace harassment, and assault. This person moved past verbal insults and into assault, and decided to treat me like garbage after surviving a near death experience. I reported harassment. Their action from mere insults had now escalated to a physical attack.

When I called to report, and said I was filing a report against another volunteer, the Security Manager said this, "Are you sure? That person could get in trouble." This was before I explained anything, before I even sent in the email or told her about anything of what the person did. I called to ask how to proceed before I had given any information. There is only one reason to ask that question, it is to dissuade volunteers from reporting, which the Peace Corps does not want and actively persecutes those who do as policy. The Peace Corps refuses to prosecute unless it is to defend their image, which is why I am sure they will come after me for writing this. In all the history of the Peace Corps, they have never prosecuted a volunteer. They have persecuted many, as there are dozens of volunteers who have spoken about this. The Peace Corps will drag my name through the dirt, they will discredit me anyway they can. The Peace Corps, as a policy, does not prosecute volunteers, even if a Peace Corps Volunteer murders another volunteer because the female volunteer refused to have sex with the male volunteer. The Peace Corps will help the murderer escape justice as they did in the case of Deborah Gardner. Prosecution goes against the Peace Corps image, so they helped a murderer escape justice. I have seen so many stories of people who reported issues, and all the Peace Corps does is persecute the reporting volunteer. The volunteer who hit me with a chair, now works for USAID. Silence is rewarded in the Peace Corps; reporting gets you persecuted.

There is no altruism in the Peace Corps. If you are being terminated in the Peace Corps, they give you 24 hours to resign your post before being terminated, and they will blame you regardless. This makes many problems go away for the bureaucracy. The Peace Corps gives you an option to report a name, and report without a name. Reporting without a name is used as a statistic that does not really do anything, and I would question the validity of those statistics. Reporting with a name carries legal responsibility, which is why the following happened. The Peace Corps, as a policy, had to silence me, so they manipulated me and threatened me. The Peace Corps does not want the accuracy of what really goes on in the Peace Corps to be known, it goes against their image.

FALLOUT

I often thought I should have died in that river. I only blamed myself after being manipulated by the Country Director. That is what victimization does to you, it makes you think it is your fault. I blamed myself for almost losing my life. The Peace Corps blames anyone they can and the dead and the volunteers are as easy to blame and cause less problems. It is the living ones that cause real problems, as a living one can speak and write. I went to Batumi to continue work on a project. I mentioned the situation to a local colleague, they acted as if they did not hear and moved on to the next task.

The Security Manager called me and told me to come to HQ as soon as possible as they wanted to have "a chat," now I knew something foul was in the wind. The Country Director works through fear and intimidation and manipulation behind closed doors, and this has happens in every Peace Corps country, there are many reports of this happening. The Peace Corps does not want to report anything and the Peace Corps does not want anything reported to Washington from the country of service. The Peace Corps tries to contain everything in country, and now I understand the mold comment from the Country Director. There are two Peace Corps, one is the domestic one in America full of smiling faces. The second is a paramilitary organization that spreads American Exceptionalism abroad, that uses fear, intimidation, and psychological manipulation on volunteers, and this is how they act. The Peace Corps is friendly and supportive in public, behind closed doors they will intimidate you into silence. Most volunteers do not speak up because it is stressful, because it is the US government, and because there are lifelong benefits to serving, like free travel, titles, and government jobs. If you want to speak out, be prepared to lose those benefits. I have already lost everything.

When I returned "home", I met a wave of hostility coming from the village. The Peace Corps sent the police and told the student to stay away from me. One of the locals blatantly called me an idiot thinking I did not speak the language. My reply, "Who are you calling an idiot?" To his shock, he backed down and walked away apologizing. There is no "home" in the Peace Corps. "Volunteer" means more to Americans than it does any other country.

Another one said, "what can't swim, he was just joking?" I turned on him and starred him down and he backed away. Any time problems arise between groups, the groups close rank and stick to their own culture, even against you if you came to help them and they almost killed you. They will seek their own social preservation over you. Human instinct will always turn to blame the outsider. Whenever the Peace Corps is in trouble with a foreign culture, they will turn on the volunteer to protect their image, because their objective is to influence the foreign culture, not protect the volunteers. Never forget, you are a foreigner, and you come last. My host father asked how I could drown, stating I was a big man. I told him he came from behind. The Peace Corps states your site is your home, never believe them, you are a foreigner and that is it. "He was just joking." My sailor nihilist friend was the sincerest, "Drowning is no joke." If anyone knows the danger of water, it is a sailor, and a nihilistic one.

There was some good that came of it, the father of the student who grabbed my hand, his father was now super proud of his son. For the first time I saw the kid smile and laugh with his father, and he kept showing off his new quarter. I never saw him happier or his father more approving, now he was publicly hugging his son for saving the American. I should have given him a dollar. There were villagers who understood.

Ivana said she wanted to murder him. One friend's father said I should have just punched the kid. I told him I was working for the government and had rules to follow. Coming from the Soviet Union, he understood. I followed the rules as written down in the Peace Corps rule book, and I was punished for it, as you will see.

OUT OF THE PAN

I was already numb by this point. Even the kid who threw up on me on the train to Tbilisi barely even registered. I took out a bottle of water and poured it over the vomit, wiped the rest away with paper towels and went back to watching the landscape. I understood why one volunteer continued drinking her coffee after she plucked a live cockroach out of her drink. Just reached in with her fingers, flung the roach to the floor and kept drinking. Many hopeful volunteers are ground down. My feelings were null. I arrived in the capital, and found my hotel room and waited for the next day, thinking about what awaited me. What you will read in the following section is not an isolated incident; many other volunteers have all reported the same thing. Targeting and abusing volunteers who report other volunteers is official policy in the Peace Corps.

INTERROGATION AND HOW THE PEACE CORPS TREATS VICTIMS

This is everything I can remember from memory, and there was more as the conversation went on for longer than this brief summary. The Peace Corps could have talked to me as a person, but they chose the path of threats, psychological manipulation, and intimidation. This is where the Peace Corps ruined my life and sent me down the path to the darkest part of my existence, and right after I almost died for them. Every volunteer is nervous about being kicked out of the Peace Corps, as that is the threat the Peace Corps uses, and they use it for any reason. The Peace Corps policy is similar to Stalin's policy, "No man, no problem." Volunteers say the best policy is to stay as far away from the administration as possible. Peace Corps Georgia has had country directors who ordered the volunteers to stay in their villages for the full two years under threat. Soldat said it best, "They will find a reason to kick you out if they don't want you." This is the pervasive thought in the Peace Corps, as when you get there, the first thing they give you is a rule book an inch thick, and you can be terminated for something as simple as driving a car or just holding a gun. Remember the story of the Asian-American volunteer, good example, anything to protect the image of the Peace Corps. The Peace Corps administration will not take any risks with their public image. The Peace Corps is never on the volunteer's side. Do not forget, you are not an employee in the Peace Corps and have no legal protections. You are a volunteer, and that is your legal definition, you have NO RIGHTS in the Peace Corps unless you sue. The Peace Corps has created a wonderful legal grey area for themselves. The Peace Corps abuses victims behind closed doors as they did me.

I showed up the next morning to HQ. I thought about the history classes I took. I thought about how the medieval diplomats carried written messages and how the envoy carried a verbal message that could not be proven, a threat or a promise. I thought about how often diplomats lie and manipulate behind closed doors. Never forget the Peace Corps is the State Department. I walked in knowing something foul waited for me, knowing what others had told me.

I walked in and the Country Director was waiting. He started to show me around the building as if I had not been there a hundred times. He was trying to lull me into being comfortable. Showed me the dozen or so rooms I had seen a dozen or so times and he talked nonchalantly about the weather. Then he took me to the Security Manager who had a nervous look on her face, which reassured me to what I already knew. Then he took me into his office, airconditioned I noticed first. He offered me a cup of water to which I said sure, and he told me to go get it myself. The Country Director would make a drowning man get himself a glass of water. He wants to instill he is in control. I found my glass of water and came back, and found him with a notepad on his knee so he could see what he wrote and I could not, but I could clearly see him when he wrote. He would only write something when I did not agree with him, or refused, and he made a show of his writing and emphasized it in an exaggerated way giving a grunt of disapproval and shaking his head frowning. He only wrote something down when I disagreed or said no about the harassment. When he wrote, I could see his hand moving, he rarely picked up his pen for word spacing. I figured he was writing in cursive. He was less than a meter away from me as he sat in one of the chairs around a little coffee table. I sat on his right, not across from him.

"I want to see what's going on with you. How's your Georgian? Rogor tqven?" He said, speaking rapidly and assertively in a manner to sound confident, which is stupid when saying "how are you?" Only one problem, at one meeting, he had said his mind could not take in any more languages, which means he did not want to study Georgian. Now he wanted to intimidate me with a language he wrote off, and his speech did not go past, "how are you?" He mentioned sometime during this interrogation, that in Georgia where over a hundred volunteers served, only seven volunteers carried on learning the language after training. I was one, despite having a teacher I did not like. Many volunteers viewed the Georgian language as a useless language, even he did not want to learn the language. Why would you expect a volunteer to learn Georgian when the Country Director refused?

"Gargad, madloba, da shen?" He switched back to English.

"What's going on?"

"What do you mean?" he became agitated at my question.

"Drowning, harassment, the fire department?"

"The fire department, what are you talking about?" That confused me.

"You called the fire department for problems with a truck." It took me a second to figure out what he was talking about. In early summer I had been sitting at a café near the main road, when an old soviet truck started up near me and was belching thick black smoke that had caused me to have an allergic reaction. I could not breathe and was coughing and wheezing for over an hour, even in the open air outside while sitting down. I was having an asthma attack or an allergic reaction. I called the Peace Corps doctors for the medical problem. The Peace Corps called the fire department which sent over a Georgian fire department official to take a report for no reason, when I called the doctors to check on my lungs for what I thought was an asthma attack. I still do not understand why the fire department came, but knowing the Peace Corps, they screwed something up. The Peace Corps will take legal action without notifying you or asking for your permission as they do not care about your permission, this has happened to other volunteers. I did not call the fire department. I called the doctors because I was having trouble breathing.

"Your office called the fire department, not me. I called medical because I was having problems breathing after an allergic reaction."

"Oh.... What about the harassment?" He looked temporarily confused before regaining his composure and wanting to move away from something he would be responsible for. He was blaming me for the actions of the Peace Corps. Peace Corps, blame the victim. It was clear he was trying to build a case against me and use any evidence he could find. I only have one question for the Peace Corps, what was he doing with my medical records? I did not call the administration for an allergic reaction; I only called the doctors.

"Did you read my report?"

"I read...something." He looked noticeably uncomfortable at the mention of the word report. I noticed a red flag here, he did not want to say the word report one way or another, he wanted to create plausible deniability that he never read anything despite the fact I filed it. He did not even want to say the word report. This is Peace Corps policy; they bury reports and act like nothing ever happens.

"Then you already know everything."

"I don't see a crime here; it could have been by mistake."

"How? The volunteer said verbatim, 'I wasn't aiming for your leg' that proves forethought for crushing my bag. Physical contact was made and registered as an attack, which is the legal definition of assault. How is this not assault? By the way, I reported harassment, which it definitely is."

He scratched the back of his head and looked away, "I'm not a lawyer." This shows he knows the law, which means his only direction was to get me to agree with him through intimidation so he would not have to report anything or terminate me. This is official policy in the Peace Corps. I like how I had to defend my reporting here, and how the other person was not even questioned at all, and nothing was done. The volunteer who did this to me was never notified about any of it. By this point I was stressed out, and whenever I disagreed with him, he started writing while shaking his head. He was using this as an intimidation tactic, he wanted this problem to be stopped here in his office, and the Peace Corps actively prevents reporting. He did not write anything down when I told him details of the incidents that took place, but only when I disagreed or refused.

"I reported harassment and not assault…"

"Stop behaving like a child!" He raged at me suddenly, slamming his fist down. The Peace Corps uses threats of violence and verbal abuse against victims. They did it to me, they will do it to you. My eye twitched uncountably as I winced away from him. He saw me wince, and my eye twitching, and he chose to continue manipulating me, he saw the state of my mind and exploited it. My eye would stay that way for over two years, twitching, long after I had left the Peace Corps. There is no excuse for this, a high-ranking Peace Corps government official treating a victim like this. This is the reality of the Peace Corps and who they really are behind closed doors. This is where I started blaming myself for everything.

Behind closed doors, the Peace Corps is filled with two-faced lying diplomats like this one, the Peace Corps is pathetic and psychopathic when it comes to their "image" and only persecutes volunteers who report. He questioned me repeatedly for close to an hour, wearing me down. At no time did he mention I could leave or anything, no rights, no nothing, I was trapped with his threats and insults, and psychological manipulation and intimidation, and the Peace Corps' threats of termination. I was panicking now, I wanted him to go away, I was afraid of him, he became aggressive towards me, and I knew there was no going away without him letting me go. At no time were any rights of victims mentioned, and no legal proceedings took place. The Peace Corps had threatened me and insulted me and humiliated me, and manipulated me after I almost died for them. The Peace Corps was not there to help me, I was alone, being abused behind closed doors by the Peace Corps. I was panicking putting up with the insults and threats of the Peace Corps. If I did not agree, he would terminate me and find some rule to say I violated, to be victim blamed. He would terminate me if I did not drop it. The Peace Corps only cares about their image. This was an interrogation by someone with military intelligence experience, meant to isolate and coerce.

"What about the drowning story?" He was now asking the victim to recount his story, when it had already been reported. I still carried on, being as open an honest as possible, still believing in the Peace Corps, and they were abusing me.

"I almost drowned. I was swimming like I normally do, saw my friend up the river and tried to catch up to him when I got jumped behind from one of my high schoolers." I felt numb and cold as I told this story again as it happened about a few days before. The drowning incident is the only part of the entire thing that I did not turn in a written report. While I was speaking about the river and almost drowning, he did not even lift his pen once, and he did not write anything down, the part where if he was actually taking notes, would have been the place to write, but he did not. "I don't know how long I was under; it was the longest time I ever held my breath. I ended up having to choke myself to stay alive. If I tried to breathe like my body wanted to, I would have drowned. I was under for a long time, longer than I thought possible. It got to the point I looked up and saw the sun thought how pretty. At this point I was motionless, no bubbles were coming out of me. I don't know why, but the pressure on my head was gone. I don't know if he was joking or trying to kill me. Or if someone else stopped him or what, I don't know. The pressure was gone, I swam up and one of my other students reached out to grab me. I gave him a quarter; I should have given him dollar." The Country Director smirked a little at the comment, and was quiet the rest of the time as I relived my story. "I was almost killed by my own student. Now the village is hostile thanks to the police showing up." Even after I explained the situation, he still carried on the manipulation and the intimidation act, but only when I refused to agree with him. He knew what happened and still carried on psychologically manipulating me.

He started talking about his time working with military intelligence. "When I was working in Afghanistan, to find Taliban insurgents, I had to take my body armor off, get out of the Humvee, and sit down with the heads of the villages in their homes to negotiate for information, man to man." He mentioned earlier he was working with the military right before the Peace Corps in an information gathering capacity. What was he doing in the Peace Corps? He was never a soldier as he said, but he sure worked with military intelligence, so why was he in Peace Corps Georgia? Then I remembered he said we were there to expand NATO. At the same time, the US military was training the Georgian military. The Peace Corps works in tandem with the US military to convert countries. Peace Corps for the civilians, military for the military, both operations are led by the same people. "You will have to go back out there to your village and finish your job, gain their trust. I had to take my body armor off to talk with them." After almost being killed by a villager, he wanted me to go back to living right beside them, the village was openly hostile thanks to the Peace Corps sending the cops. If the village complained at all, I would be blamed and terminated, even though they tried to kill me. He did not even mention moving to another site which they can do easily, to a site that did not have a history of trying to drown me. He wanted everything to remain the same, no reports. A few weeks before, another volunteer in my region was assaulted by a Georgian and moved to a different site, no legal action was taken. The volunteer was moved because it was not safe, so why was he sending me back? He did not want to report anything. "Speaking of which, how is home?" He asked the red flag question. He was trying to trick me after I almost died, was being manipulated by him, and he decided to test me about home?

"Which home?" I asked.

"Good answer, I meant America?" He was being deceptive.

I had not spoken to my family or friends in America since before the river. I was tearing up and stuttering when I tried to talk about my friends and missing weddings and other important events. I had not stuttered in years. I could not even say a sentence I was stuttering so badly at this point. When I looked over at him, his face was contorted in disgust, he was glaring at me, judging me for missing friends and family while serving and after a traumatic experience. Here I was reliving a traumatic event, explaining everything in detail, and sharing my personal life, and he was judging me for it. He scowled at a victim of his program. This is the leadership of the Peace Corps behind closed doors: judging a man for missing his friends after a life-threatening experience while serving in a foreign country. Here I was reliving my own victimization and being treated like dirt by a Peace Corps Country Director, "I missed my best friend's wedding, I've missed a lot." I thought I should have died; I was out here trying to make the world a better place, and all it got me was nearly killed by the people I came to help, and this Peace Corps bureaucrat was giving me dirty looks while I spoke. I never felt more alone in my life. I know my friends would have been crushed by my death. I felt guilty for putting my own life at risk to serve America. The fact the Peace Corps downplays volunteers dying in the Peace Corps is another contributor to that guilt. I already blamed myself and now the Peace Corps was dumping more onto me. They do not want to advertise the risk in serving. I felt guilty about almost being killed. Here I was being revictimized by a Peace Corps Country Director. If they cared about volunteers, why was I treated like this? The Peace Corps hates victims because it goes against their image.

"And with your host family?"

"Food is causing me health problems; things are fine with the family."

"Well, everything is fine then, and about the other thing, just move on, move on, just move on," his face turned friendly, the sudden change from disgusted to friendly only told me it was a manipulation. His hand flicked like he was saying no to mashed potatoes at thanksgiving, same movement. Physically gesturing to move on as he said. "Just move on. Just move on." This is coercion.

"No, I ..."

He cut me off by grunting loudly in disgust, shaking his head, scowling, and immediately started writing something on his paper. By this point I had been sitting there for close to an hour dealing with his abuse, reliving the trauma, going over everything. I was broken. He was manipulating me into silence, and it works, abusing a victimized person makes them easy to force them to agree with you. Imagine that, interrogating, intimidating, and abusing a victim works, proven by the Peace Corps. He could ruin my life by terminating me and no one would ask questions, and what could I do, I was a volunteer and signed up for this. Psychologically twisted and tortured by the CIA while in the Peace Corps, right after I almost died for them.

I wanted him to leave me alone. It was nothing for him to manipulate me. What he had done to get information in Afghanistan, he now used against victims in the Peace Corps. Not through any of this interrogation did he ever mention any rights, laws, or even the fact I could go or did not have to say anything. I was trapped by him and could not leave, or else, they would terminate me. This is a real threat from the Peace Corps. Volunteers have put their life on hold to serve their country, and to be terminated can ruin your career and life, and prevent you from receiving the benefits from your service. The Peace Corps knows this. The Peace Corps conditions volunteers to think this is the most important job on earth, and then they use the threat of termination to keep volunteers in line. It is one giant psych job, and I volunteered for it.

I was broken down and scared, panicking. I grabbed the chair and pushed myself back into the seat I was so scared of being attacked by him, I was having a panic attack. Being verbally and emotionally abused, manipulated, after almost dying for your country by people that are supposed to be there to support you, destroys your mind. He knew what was going on with me, he could see my eye twitching at his insults and struggling emotionally. He did not care. Then I blurted out in fear and panic the words I will regret the rest of my life, "I'm sorry," I yelled it, terrified. And that was the last time I will ever apologize for anything. Here I was being interrogated, abused, and manipulated by military intelligence in the Peace Corps. Here I was, the one almost killed for my country by the people I came to help, being called a child by a man living in luxury, hit by a volunteer while trying to heal, apologizing for it all.

He smiled a sickening grin I will remember the rest of my life, I felt like a whore. I felt sick, I had been manipulated by him. I was broken by the Peace Corps, to be fair though, it was an interrogation, intimidation, psychological manipulation, abuse, and threats against a victim. My service to America meant more to me than my life to me, and they have kicked out people for far less. Notice how he never said any direct threats, only glaring at me, shaking his head, writing, it is an implied threat, they do everything to avoid legal responsibility in the Peace Corps, and they take it to extreme measures. They will do this to you. Imagine, a manipulative high ranking government official using intimidation and coercion in the Peace Corps to silence a victim. I lived it. It is easier for them to kick you out and far less damaging to the public image of the Peace Corps. The image of the Peace Corps is the only thing the Peace Corps cares about. It is propaganda. After all of this, it cannot be denied.

He let out a long breath and leaned back in his chair. He tossed the notepad down on the table less than two feet in front of me, no longer concerned with the charade. "Ok, there's nothing to worry about." He rubbed the back of his head and looked up at something as if to figure out what was next.

While he looked up and away, I leaned in and looked at the notepad he threw down. It landed face up and facing me so I could read it easily, as he tossed it onto the table in front of me, carelessly. When he threw it, it he flicked his wrist a little, enough for the paper to turn 90 degrees facing me. I leaned in and studied it. Immediately one thing was clear, there were no words on the page, there was scribbling, but no words. It was all a manipulation by a Peace Corps Country Director. The paper in front of me was a white legal pad and on it were four lines of scribbling at the top third of the page. From a distance, it would have looked like four long words, spaced out evenly. Close up, I could see it clearly. Each scribble was one unbroken twisted line of blocky inky waves in a repeating pattern, the scribbles themselves were an inch to two inches apart from each other. Over 90% of the page was blank. It was not writing, not cursive, not short hand, not even notes in his bad handwriting, it looked nothing like cursive English. He squiggled to make it look like he was writing something down to intimidate me. It was clear as daylight in front of me. I have read his handwriting before; I have even translated medieval Latin handwriting seven hundred years old. What was on that legal pad was what you would find in place of writing to make it look like something was written down from afar. It was easy for me to see less than two feet from my face as I leaned in and had a good long look at it. It was an interrogation trick cops use to get a confession, intimidate a suspect by writing something unknown, and he used it against me. He already knew what he wanted, and he knew how to get it. This nonverbal, behind closed doors manipulation tactic has to end, and every volunteer needs to know what the Peace Corps does, they manipulate people. Taking away one weapon or manipulative tactic from the Peace Corps and the US government would be a victory.

When he turned his head towards me again, he saw me looking at the paper, and as I looked up at him, his eyes went wide, and then he grabbed the paper and flipped it face down on his lap. He put his hand on my knee changing his demeanor, "You trust me, right?" he said with a smile. His demeanor changing to the exact opposite from seconds before. Never trust the Peace Corps, they are liars and manipulators.

I replied in kind, "yes sir." My mind was reduced to being a gibbering idiot. I was broken as a man, "Am I in trouble sir?"

"No, at least not from my side, however you will have to go back and win the trust of the village. Come on, let's go get those lungs looked at." After an hour of abuse and manipulation, he walked away like it did not even matter and it was all part of the job of being a Peace Corps Country Director. Only after did I apologize, did his demeanor change, into a normal person, before he was aggressive and hostile, now he was like a normal person. It is all a mask. Only after I apologized did he let me go. I was never the same.

DOCTOR VRACH

He walked me down to the doctor's office and as soon as he left, I broke down crying in front of the doctor. She had to give me drugs to calm me down. Emotionally I was broken and gone as a person; and this was the direct result of the actions of the Peace Corps, it was only after his actions of his abuse and manipulation. Doctor Vrach, I had trusted for a long time by this point, as she was a genuine person. I do not know her relationship to the Country Director. There is a divide between the doctors and the administration, as they have different laws that govern them both, look for the distance. You do not want to see a Peace Corps doctor being close with a country director. After being verbally and psychologically abused by the Country Director, I broke down shaking, my entire body went into tremors and could not stop. I had no faith in any of the system, or the mission, and that is what broke me, an interrogation of a victim. I was broken. Vrach was shocked. I could not stop shaking. I was crying. She was a comforting person, but I was in a psychological hell.

"What is the most important thing?"

I looked up, "I am alive?" I guessed.

"Good."

She told me to breathe in and out slowly. It did not help me calm down. I was crying, and panicking. This is the end result of abuse and manipulation. This is the end result of the Peace Corps policy of silencing reports. This is the reality of the Peace Corps behind the image.

She began to examine me, noting the bruises on my arms and legs from where I clambered onto the rocks from the river. I did not even notice the bruises. "I'm sorry but you are a victim." Declared a victim by the US government, manipulated and abused by the Peace Corps.

I broke down crying even more. I never felt more alone. I was shaking uncontrollably. She gave me anti-anxiety pills that are a controlled substance in Georgia. I took them every half hour. When I took a sip of water, I started coughing. If I am not paying attention when I take a drink, my throat will slam shut subconsciously. It was a reflex from drowning. The doctor gave me another pill as I ended up spitting the last one out onto the floor inadvertently. She calmed me down enough to send me to the medical hotel.

She gave me pills and told me to wait for further instructions. The longer I waited the worse my shaking became. I took the pills every thirty minutes, waiting for the second. I remember waiting in the room, feeling the most alone I ever felt in my life. I sat there alone shaking, thinking. What is the point of this? Is this worth it? Are they going to throw me out? I almost died serving my country only to be abused. The Peace Corps image is all about world peace and building an international community. Here I was alone, shaking uncontrollably after being manipulated and abused by military intelligence. I asked myself, "What is the point of serving America? What is the point of the Peace Corps?" I had no answer.

Doctor Vrach called. She asked me if I wanted to keep serving. The most important question they would keep asking me. I said yes. She asked me if I wanted to go to America for treatment. I asked her what she would do because I did not know. She said it might be better for me, get everything looked at and get treatment for my other medical problems. I said OK.

A Peace Corps psychologist from Washington called me next. I reported the incident when it happened, but only five days later did anyone do anything, after the country director abused me. To get psychological help in the Peace Corps, you have to be broken down and shaking, and then it is for only 45 days. Why did they wait till I was broken down and needed pills to stop shaking days later? Why did they wait? I reported it? Was someone sitting on the report, not letting me get the help I needed? I was shaking only after the Country Director and his abuse. They did not answer my questions. I was being sent to America.

I did not sleep well. I returned to the village to pack. I loaded up my bags, and piled everything into my suitcases. I met up with Ivana and spoke to her one last time. She was shocked I was leaving. I knew I was not coming back. Ivana revealed something to me. The Peace Corps Volunteer before me had been sexually assaulted in my village, and she did not report it. She was afraid to be moved to a different site as Ivana said. The village was not safe to start with, no village is. Crimes go unreported in the Peace Corps. Everything goes unreported in the Peace Corps, as the Peace Corps actively buries reports and abuses those who report them. This is the reality behind the Peace Corps image.

The next morning, I said goodbye to my host father who thought I was going on vacation. I said goodbye to Maria's family, they were sad. The taxi came. I ordered the taxi to stop near the restaurant. I hopped out and ran into the restaurant to say goodbye to Aksana. I hugged her goodbye; she was sad. She thanked me for being her friend and studying together. In the blink of an eye, I was gone. I had to leave my friends behind.

I was still shaking as I returned to Tbilisi. I had limited time left so I called Lisa, to say goodbye. She dropped everything and came over and we went to see a movie together. The Country Director saw the same movie at the same theater at the same time. He had to come over to say hello. He was trying to smile like he was friendly. I had never seen a bureaucrat-diplomat nervous before. When diplomats are behaving friendly, that is when they are weak. This time he was worried, I could read it on his face.

Lisa and I said our goodbyes and she handed me gift, a little soviet star. The only medal I would ever get from serving America. There are no medals in the Peace Corps. I thanked her and placed it in my backpack. I called Soldat, Druggie, and Mjolnir. Soldat was supportive, they all were. They hoped to see me come back, but that was a question I could not answer. Before Lisa left, she turned and gave me a kiss, "Tell them what happened." After midnight, I went to the airport. I turned down the doctor's escort offer knowing others needed medical support more than me. A medical escort would take up to four days of the doctor's time, full trip, putting the program on one doctor. Two doctors for over a hundred people on 24-hour call. I travelled back to America by myself.

AIR TRAVEL

I know what it means to be beside myself. I waited alone in the airport for a long time. The last time I would serve in the Peace Corps in-country was in the airport waiting for a psychological med-evac alone. It was late in the night. I looked around wondering how I had gotten here, what events had to transpire. I had a long time to think. A long time to sit alone with my bags as my only companion. There would be no closing ceremony for me and my service. I never found closure for what happened in the Peace Corps.

By the time I came to our capital, I was exhausted and emotionally gone, both by the emotional trauma, and by the transition stateside. My mind was gone. The Victim's Response Unit woman picked me up and took me back to her office and handed me money for food. Then she took me to my hotel room, she was a nice lady who would threaten me later. She was surprised when I said I did not have a smartphone and needed a phone. The Peace Corps expects you to have your own smartphone, even the doctors expect you to use our own phone and not the one the Peace Corps provides. She had to put in a special order for a phone as they did not have a spare one for evacuated volunteers. After me, the Peace Corps had spare phones in case someone like me comes along. I did change the Peace Corps; victims can get phones now. I guess I was one of the few that was not wealthy. I came from nothing and everything

I have, I worked for myself. They were not prepared for that. She was a polite woman, she told me they had problems with this Country Director before, and had reports on him. She suggested I report him to the Inspector General. They had reports on him and let this happen. I wonder why? Let us ask about those reports.

She took me to my hotel room and told me there was grocery store nearby. I was already undergoing reverse culture shock. I walked to the grocery store. I walked in, and saw all the choices, every single food product, thousands of items on the shelves. I left the grocery store and went back to my hotel room and broke down. I could not even process the grocery store; it was too much. I had been living on almost nothing for so long in a tiny room with no freedom. There were too many choices. I could not even think about anything, there was too much of everything. I sat in my room and tried to sleep; I woke up from nightmares. My first day in America, the first time I ate in America, I went to the buffet at the hotel and made myself waffles. I broke down crying into them. They tasted so amazing compared to the food I had been living off of. They were cheap hotel waffles. I was still having stomach problems.

MEDICAL EVACUATION

D.C.

I know what white privilege is because of what I saw in Washington DC. Non-white Peace Corps Volunteers are not considered American by foreigners. In DC, I saw the same thing. There was one Peace Corps Volunteer who was med-evaced the same time as myself. She served in the military and was Honorably Discharged, and then she joined the Peace Corps. She was a kind and wonderful human being. I have a lot of respect for her, and as I usually do, I thanked her for her service to America as a veteran, as I did with all veterans. I found out what happened to her from another volunteer, who volunteered the information. I do not ask. No good volunteer asks why someone is medically evacuated.

She was raped in the Peace Corps. By who? I never found out and I did not ask. If she wanted to talk, I would have listened, but I was not going to pry. The ultimate sacrifice is not dying for your country, it is being raped for it, and she was punished for trying to help the world. Rape is a serious problem in the Peace Corps. She was a middle-eastern American, wore a hijab, and was Muslim. She prayed regularly and was devout in her faith. Having not missed a Sunday of church in twenty years, I had respect for her.

All of what I saw happened while she was serving America, because when a volunteer is med-evaced, they are still on duty in the Peace Corps. While she was still serving her country, and after being raped, the proud white people of DC were giving her dirty looks, calling her names, and they looked down on her. Another volunteer who was black and wore an African equivalent of the Hijab, experienced the same thing. Being a white male, I did not see it until it was pointed out to me by the black volunteer. You have to be there and see it. The Muslim volunteer never reacted, never pointed it out, she took the abuse in silence. I am thankful I met both of them, or else I would have never seen how racist America really is. This was the most important lesson I learned from the Peace Corps. You do not see it until it is pointed in your direction. It was racism aimed directly at the people who served and sacrificed the most for America, from those who benefited the most from that service and that sacrifice.

I wanted to throw up, I still do, thinking my service benefitted these bigots. Imagine how the Muslim volunteer felt. I heard this from the volunteer who wore an African head cover from the country she served in. It was nothing but racial and anti-Islamic slurs for them, through their medevac. When I was with them, I watched it occur. When there is a white male with them, there was less hostility than when they were by themselves, but I still saw the dirty looks and the head turns. The Peace Corps says white males have to look out for minorities and women in the Peace Corps while serving, I did not expect that to mean in Washington DC as well. The black volunteer, she had been in a horrible accident and had to have multiple surgeries while serving. She was covered in stitches and bandages. She was on her way out as her 45 days were up. Her main fear was the post medical care after Peace Corps. She was worried about the surgeries she needed and how volunteers do not receive treatment or they are treated like dirt by the Department of Labor, and the Peace Corps does not care. The Peace Corps screwed her on her medical care. I would soon learn of this problem.

For everything the Muslim Volunteer had been through, she was putting up a strong face of strength. No one wants to talk about rape in the Peace Corps, which makes me think it is far more common than the statistics represent. Sexual assault is far more prevalent than what the numbers show, I know that for a fact. From some of the articles I have read, rape victims have even been victim blamed by the Peace Corps. The Peace Corps does not care about victims in the least. Victims go against their image.

MED-EVAC HOTEL

You have two options for treatment, go home or to DC. You have 45 days to heal before they kick you out. The Peace Corps has part of a hotel on contract, whether there are med-evac volunteers or not. The first person I met was a woman around 22. Everyone is curious about why everyone is there. I never asked anyone why they were there. She told me she was having an abortion. As she said, she was in training with her American boyfriend and he did not care to put on a condom. In order to stay and finish her service to the Peace Corps, she was forced to have an abortion and then return to her country of service. I wished her a quick recovery. She looked nervous mentioning the word abortion. I did not want to add to her stress. Even as a devout Catholic, I still believe a woman has a right to her own body.

Never feel bad about being med-evaced. Other volunteers I met had minor medical issues the Peace Corps could not treat in country, and there is a long list of what the Peace Corps cannot do in country. Medical treatment for volunteers is extremely limited in country. I was still living with back pain, ankle pain, stomach pain, and everything else that happened. The other volunteers showed me photos of their service in other continents. They were living in apartments by themselves, all on their Peace Corps stipend. These spacious beautiful apartments, with amazing views and they were paid in dollars. Here I was, living in a closet, getting paid in Lari, forced to eat potatoes that were eating away at my insides. Georgia was a great example of cheapness in the Peace Corps.

There was only one person I have ever met who used drugs while in the Peace Corps. He smoked pot in his room every day and everyone could smell it through the vents, it stank up everyone's rooms. I was questioned when a Peace Corps nurse came to check on me and smelled the pot. I told her it was someone else in the hotel, and it was coming through the vents. She sighed and understood it was not me after she smelled the vent. She smelled the same thing in other rooms. I had never done any drugs in my life by this point. I have the delightful memory of him telling me, "You're here because you were playing", which is a great way to treat a victim, blame the victim to their face. Even volunteer's victim blame, if it is good enough for the Peace Corps, it is good enough for the volunteer. He was a great example of how hateful some volunteers can be. Psychological issues are taboo in the American culture and in the Peace Corps. No one in the Peace Corps wants to address it, because if they do, they will have to pay for it and state people can have psychological issues stemming from the Peace Corps. This goes against their image. Join the Peace Corps, get PTSD, no one would join.

A GRIM LOBBY

It was a haunting feeling; I was standing in the lobby of the Peace Corps building. The memorial for the Peace Corps Volunteers who died in service is in the lobby. It is a little taller than a person, and made of four or five black slabs with the names of every volunteer who died engraved on it. I remember standing there and reading the names on the wall, every single one of them row by row, not knowing what happened. My name almost went up there, a few more seconds and my entire story would have been summed up in black granite, another name on the wall. That is what dying in the Peace Corps gets you, a few inches of black rock.

At the time, I blamed myself for everything and thought it would have been better had I ended up on the wall. I blamed myself for so much, the drowning, even the abuse of the Country Director, and now a medevac. I know now that is a victim's mentality. I didn't even feel human, I was just a victim. I could not connect with anyone, I was isolated. Now I know what self-blame is, and what victims go through. I felt haunted around that memorial, like I somehow cheated it. The memorial for the Peace Corps needs to be placed in the National Mall.

DOCTORS

I was taken to meet the nurse in charge of my case. The first thing she said was, "Don't fall apart on me, so many volunteers come here and their bodies fall apart at the seams." I had so many physical medical problems beyond what I have written here. They do not care and will push you away from reporting medical problems. Many of the medical problems that volunteers have during service goes untreated, and that the medical care in the Peace Corps is inadequate in the extreme. The Peace Corps' only real medical focus is to treat symptoms for two years, get the volunteers in and out of country as fast and as cheap as possible. Once the volunteer is out of the Peace Corps, all the medical problems are no longer the responsibility of the Peace Corps. Your medical problems do not matter to the Peace Corps, money is more important than your life, despite you risking your life and time for free. This is the reality behind the image.

The medical situation in the Peace Corps can be summed up by the phrase "just wait, it will go away." The pain will go away, or the volunteer will. Once the volunteer out of the Peace Corps, the volunteer is no longer the Peace Corps' problem. The staff does not care, it is a bureaucracy. The medical care is terrible and they only pretend to care for 45 days, then it is not their problem. They have to wait 45 days, where you may end up waiting years for your medical problems to be solved, this is Peace Corps medical care. One Peace Corps doctor refused to give treatment to a volunteer, claiming the patient was whining, and the patient died, this is the level of care. This makes sense, as my own digestive track was being eroded away, with inflamed and swollen organs, and I was living in pain. I was having stomach pain daily. I had worn holes through sweaters from constant rubbing to dull the pain. Polyps were growing inside me, and yet I was never given a diagnosis, and never treated. The problem was the food I was living on and that was fine for them. Even though I was back in America and on American food, the damage was already done and I needed multiple surgeries. They didn't care. Me risking cancer was fine for the Peace Corps. The sprained ankle I had and my back injury never healed, and only remained injured. My medical problems were never taken care of. If they do anything to help you, they treat it like they are doing you a favor. This is the attitude of the Peace Corps in DC.

For my digestive track problems, the Peace Corps sent me to a doctor who misdiagnosed the whole thing, saying it was a bone issue and not my stomach. Then when I still complained about my stomach pain, the Peace Corps nurse told me, "Oh, it's just a dietary thing and in a few weeks on American food, your stomach pain will go away." It never did, and continued to cause me pain to the point I needed multiple surgeries. At the end of a few weeks, they sent me home with no further action done by the Peace Corps, no diagnosis, and no concern by the Peace Corps. I ended up requiring multiple surgeries. I would receive a surgery a year after being discharged, two years after I first complained of the problem. Because of my Peace Corps service, I had to have multiple surgeries on my digestive track, from issues originating from my service in the Peace Corps. My body was wrecked. One surgery I had to pay for all by myself thanks to the Peace Corps. All of my medical problems were so blatantly obvious, but no one diagnosed it.

What type of medical expert says, "just wait, it will go away." Just wait, a great way to delay someone until they are not your problem, that is the Peace Corps, delay until they are discharged. Only Peace Corps medical personnel would tell someone their medical problems will go away on their own. The Peace Corps is nothing but government bureaucrats.

Peace Corps, treating the symptom since 1961. Funny, how the Peace Corps "helps" the poor of other countries is the same as their medical care, they only treat the symptom of the problem, but not to effect actual change. That would undermine the whole economic colonial empire. Make it look like we are helping without fixing the problem.

I liked the doctors in Peace Corps Georgia, but they did not do anything to diagnosis or find a solution to the problem. The problem is with Peace Corps policy in DC. The Peace Corps does not want to give volunteers the medical attention they require, as it is costly and requires volunteers to be sent back to America for surgery and medical care. Money is more important than world peace, according to the Peace Corps. It is better to risk the volunteer's health and keep them in country until they are dying or dead. All the Peace Corps wants, is for you to go in, make America look great and leave quietly. It is bureaucratic propaganda. That "image" is the main reason the Peace Corps exists. When I returned to Ohio, I found a doctor who diagnosed my problem correctly on the first day and recommended surgery.

I finally had a chance to go to physical therapy, a year after the injury. The therapist was friendly, but missed the actual problem, nerve damage. I did therapy to strengthen my back but it remained numb. My ankle required more time to heal as I had been walking on an injured ankle for a year, in a place where it is easy to reinjure. I did every single stretch they gave me, and I followed every order. I was actively working on healing my body, I wanted to get better, and I was doing everything the doctors were telling me to do. I was still serving in the Peace Corps and giving it my best. The Peace Corps nurse even thanked me for doing everything I did, and commented on how easier it was to treat me while in DC than other volunteers who went home.

PSYCHOLOGIST

I met with the psychologist. The first thing she said was that my case was odd, "usually people in your situation aren't sent back here, they may receive a month of phone therapy, it's odd to be sent back." They didn't even call me until after the Country Director abused me. I told her about everything, the drowning, the volunteer, and the Country Director's interrogation. She nodded her head cautiously, weighing my words, almost as if to say, "that would do it." She said this, "Well, we will only focus on the drowning, as that's all we have time for." The doctor did not want to come close to even talking about the Country Director's actions or have anything to do with that legal responsibility. Even the Peace Corps Psychologist was a trained bureaucrat looking out for her pension. She avoided linking any responsibility to the Peace Corps, and instead chose to blame me. Peace Corps psychologists are bureaucrats first, doctors second.

    I told the doctor I saw a man who looked like the Country Director and I had panic attack with a racing heartrate, and had to pause to breathe and calm myself down. The doctor told to me to get back to the drowning topic, ignoring the problem. Whenever I mentioned anything, nightmares related to the Country Director or anything like that, she ignored it and told me to focus on the drowning. This is the treatment of a Peace Corps psychologist. What I remember the most about the Doctor, is her telling me in session, "you filed assault against a volunteer who hit you with a chair. You shouldn't have reported." A Peace Corps psychologist blaming the victim, what a testament to her profession. After I was manipulated and abused by the Country Director, she excused him and victim blamed me. Even the doctors will tell volunteers to not report anything, this is how ingrained the policy is in the Peace Corps. She said this at the beginning and at the end of our time together.

"I reported harassment doctor, not assault. By the way, that action fits the legal definition of assault." They were the ones who said assault.

"Well...I'm not a lawyer." It was the second time I heard that from a government officer, the first being the Country Director, and then it came from the psychologist who was supposed to help me. The Peace Corps Motto: "I'm not a lawyer." The battle cry of every bureaucrat looking out for their pension. Never forget, the Peace Corps is just another bureaucracy.

"Neither am I, so stick to psychology and not your legal advice."

The Doctor in our first session walked me around showing me the building, even the board of directors' conference room, which was a floor up on the top floor. The Doctor said something which I found interesting, "We don't like to go to the top floor. We like to stay on the medical floor and keep out of sight from the politics." Peace Corps employees are kept in line by fear of losing their position. They are government employees following a political appointee, nothing more. The Peace Corps says they are apolitical; what they mean is that they do not care about republicans or democrats. The Peace Corps is extremely political, just not domestically.

I met with her several times a week, writing out events, and doing paper work. It seemed like they wanted bureaucratic proof I was trying to move forward. I did the work. It helped a little. The doctor shared information with me that most are not privy to. I listened to her. She explained how being a Peace Corps psychologist made her stop watching horror movies. She used to love them. By the time I met her, she had seen far too many rape and battery victims, and dealt with all the horror the Peace Corps buries under a nice smile. As she spoke, her Peace Corps smile fell off, that mask of niceness they all wear faded, she was pulled back into a certain memory, her eyes defocused for a brief second and her face went neutral. She had a flashback. She shook herself out of it. I saw the symptoms, this doctor was exhausted, good at wearing her mask, but she was burnt out. The doctor smiled at me, but realized she had revealed far too much. I did not push, only listened. Now I know. Perhaps the only good thing to come out of all this, I know much more about the Peace Corps than the average volunteer ever will.

We met many times a week and discussed everything except the Country Director, despite my wish to discuss it. The Doctor was impressed with my efforts and wrote about my progress positively, about the drowning part that is. She was fascinated with me diving back into the river the following day. "Swimming was so important to you, you said no to fear and dived right back in so you wouldn't lose it."

"I'm not much for horses, but I know how to climb back on after falling off." It was a sign of a mentally healthy mind. I had the feeling she did not care about my case. Who would in a Peace Corps world filled with rape victims?

Her diagnosis was evident when she said, "You sound like a normal volunteer."

DO NOT PASS GO

The Peace Corps Psychologist diagnosed me healed and mentally fit for service in the Peace Corps. The US government declared me psychologically sound of mind to serve in the Peace Corps. According to the US government I am mentally fit to serve world peace. I had flashbacks and grew anxious in relation to anyone who held a position of authority over me. They declared me mentally fit to return to duty.

The Peace Corps rubber stamped me. They did the minimum for legal responsibility, to make it look like they were helping. They sent me to America for treatment to cover themselves after the Country Director's abuse, and they did everything to avoid discussing that topic. NO ONE WOULD COME CLOSE TO DISCUSSING IT WHEN I BROUGHT IT UP. The Peace Corps employees treated me like a leper on that topic. Anyone I mentioned it to, they all quickly changed the conversation, doctors, psychologist, the Victim's Response Unit, even the Inspector General's office did not want to discuss it. They diagnosed me as fit for duty, despite the nightmares and my heart racing when I saw someone who looked like the Country Director. The Peace Corps psychologist even said this at our last session, "When you came here, you didn't even want to be in the same room alone with the country director. How productive is that in a relationship with your director?" I still do not, even to this day, he is an abusive manipulator who threatens victims. I told her what happened, and she victim blamed me telling me, "You shouldn't have reported anything", as if that makes his actions acceptable. The Peace Corps shifts blame to the victim any chance they get. The Peace Corps supports abusive relationships and victim blames. The volunteer does not matter, only the image. The Peace Corps psychologist did everything to protect the Country Director, and used it against me every single time I mentioned it. I stopped talking about it, because all she did was blame me for it or skirt the issue. She did not even mention speaking to the Inspector General, only the Victim Response Unit mentioned that. The psychologist was clearly on the side of the Peace Corps and not the patient in her care. The Victim's Response Unit told me I did not have to be in the same room alone with the Country Director, then the psychologist used that against me when I said I did not want to be in the same room alone with him.

I was still in shock after being moved from world to world and dealing with thousands of adjustment issues and the previous traumas. Those 45 days are short, and there is no way that will fix every problem. The Peace Corps only allows 45 days, and then kicks you out, and they will not do anything to help you get medical care after your service. The Peace Corps does not care at all about volunteers, especially Returned Peace Corps Volunteers. 45 days is the bare minimum for their legal responsibility. There is no post-service care in the Peace Corps, and if you have any problems from your service, they are your problems and the Peace Corps victim blames you for what they caused. 45 days is all you get, then nothing. The Peace Corps does this to avoid legal responsibility. The only reason I received psychological help at all was because I was abused and psychologically manipulated by a Peace Corps country director to the point of needing drugs to stop shaking, and then they avoided that topic and declared me psychologically healthy.

The Peace Corps denied my return to service as I still needed physical therapy and had problems requiring multiple surgeries. The Peace Corps will only send you back to your country of service if you are like a brand-new volunteer in perfect health. The Peace Corps psychologist declared me psychologically fit to avoid any legal responsibility associated with the Country Director, and then they discharged me for my medical problems to get rid of me. They told me to wait to get rid of me, to deny me on my return and to cheat me on health care. You cannot trust the Peace Corps, they operate behind closed doors, and they will do anything to avoid legal responsibility.

The Peace Corps told me I could reapply. The Peace Corps denies people for any history of mental illness, even something as small as depression. Their offer was a lie. I still needed psychological help for the abuse of the country director, I need multiple surgeries, and the Peace Corps sent me home when I was still in pain and needed surgery. They sent me home without insurance. Instead of help, I received a medical discharge and was stuck with the bill. I had been living with these problems for over a year and needed help, and when the Peace Corps saw it was easier for them, they kicked me out and told me it was my problem. The Peace Corps is propaganda.

I was in perfect health when I joined the Peace Corps. I never received help from the Peace Corps for my medical problems once they discharged me. I needed surgery. My eye still twitched and it would for years. I had flashbacks. Even after all the work I did, I was still having problems dealing with people who looked like the Peace Corps Country Director, or anyone with a position of authority over me. My eye was still twitching and I had anxiety and a racing heartrate. Even to this day my back is still numb in the spot where I hit the cement. When I found work after the Peace Corps, whenever I was around anyone who was a supervisor, I became extremely anxious around them, to the point of fear, and I wanted to get away from them. This never happened before. Now I was afraid to be around anyone with a position of authority over me. This would sabotage my career and life and cause me to have flashbacks, causing me to have mental break downs while working, preventing me from being able to work. I could no longer function and was unable to build relationships at any job. The actions of the Peace Corps ruined my life and my career, shattered my self-image, and left me a broken man after I almost gave my life for them.

I did not have a problem with supervisors before, even when I worked retail which I did for years. I graduated at the top of my class from one of America's most difficult universities and built healthy relationships with all of my professors. Where I was once a devout Catholic and connected to my church community, I no longer believed in God and no longer trusted anyone. The psychologist repeatedly refused to talk about it, let alone treat it, a great example of failure in the Peace Corps. I was unable to build relationships with people around me and I felt isolated for years. I still do. I was anxious around people, waiting to be hit, waiting to be abused and lied to. I was a victimized by the Peace Corps. Relationship building was taken from me, by the Peace Corps; the very thing the Peace Corps is supposed to do, it ruined in me. Psychologically fit for duty, what a joke. I became unable to work in America, unable to function, unable to build relationships with people around me.

Mental health issues are ignored and treated taboo in the Peace Corps. They are taboo because it reveals that the Peace Corps does not care, it reveals what they really are. Two doctors on call, night and day for over a hundred people. I used to say the Peace Corps does not have enough resources to take care of all the volunteers. The Peace Corps is the US government. The Government and the Peace Corps do not care, they want cheap effective propaganda. Psychological care in the Peace Corps is a joke. You cannot trust the doctors who might just decide to terminate you. Saying the word "suicide" is an immediate medical discharge, no questions asked, and you will never be let back in. If you do talk to the doctors, it goes on your medical record for the government and bans you from the Peace Corps for life.

These same doctors can medically eject you from the Peace Corps if they find out that you had any previous mental health issues, even something as small as depression in high school. No one with a mental health history is allowed in the Peace Corps. It is exactly the same as the "Don't Ask, Don't Tell" policy for the LGBTQ community in the military in the 90's. To get into the Peace Corps, you have to disclose everything to the medical doctors who review your application. Anything you put down for the psychological health will ban you from the Peace Corps for life. If they find out you had anything, they will ban you for life from serving. I am Returned Peace Corps Volunteer, with all rights and benefits, but they would never let me back in, because of the problems I had while I served. Writing this is a suicide letter for a Returned Peace Corps

Volunteer. They will ban me for life, and take away my benefits, and ruin the rest of my life, all to defend their image.

I have to do this because the Peace Corps harms its volunteers and someone needs to expose them for their crimes. I do this to find closure, because I cannot walk away from almost dying for my country, being humiliated and manipulated and broken by the Peace Corps I served. I am not doing this for anything other than to expose the problems in the Peace Corps. Profits from this book are going to help the country I came to serve, and other NGO's and non-profit organizations. I have met many volunteers who have survived horrible crimes, like rape, and had psychological problems from the trauma; they did not put anything down on their record yet they still went on to successfully serve, even with a history of psychological problems.

All Peace Corps employees, including doctors, are looking out for their pensions before the volunteers. In the Peace Corps, in the training, they tell you to not reveal anything about your medical history. If they find out you have previous psychological problems, they will immediately terminate you and ban you. This is why so many do not speak up; lifelong benefits mean life long silence. I am sacrificing everything to write this, and I am not even getting paid.

CLOSE OF SERVICE / PUNCHLINE

The Victim Response Unit woman had me meet up with her to discuss ending my service. I was medically evacuated for something only to be medically terminated for a different reason. The Country Director reported the chair incident to his regional supervisor who said no crime had been committed to no one's surprise. The Country Director did this after I had been medically evacuated, he did this to cover himself. I should have known better than to report harassment; I mean after all, a male volunteer in the Peace Corps murdered a female volunteer because she refused to have sex, and the Peace Corps helped the murderer. The Peace Corps actively helped a woman murdering criminal escape justice. If the Peace Corps is fine with the murder of its volunteers over sex, then what merit did my complaint of being hit with a chair have? The Peace Corps does not believe in feminism, it is another lie. For the Peace Corps, harassment and murder are equally acceptable. The Peace Corps will do anything to protect their image, which means they will have to destroy me any way they can.

The Peace Corps' Victim Response Unit, the woman in charge of handling victims immediately after victimization, threatened me. Behind closed doors, she told me this: "I asked my superior about your situation.

If you take us to court over this, we will press criminal charges against you." That is what the Peace Corps told me after I almost died for them. The Peace Corps threatened me after I almost died for their cause. She was referring to the events that took place in the Country Director's office, and she was carrying the threat from her superior. The Peace Corps' Victim Response Unit threatens victims into silence, all in order to protect their image. The only thing that matters to the Peace Corps is the image. If the Peace Corps image requires threatening victims into silence to survive, then it is only propaganda.

The Peace Corps' response to victims is to threaten them. The Peace Corps is a joke for how their Victim's Unit treats victims, threatening victims of their cause with legal action in order to silence them. This is what they did to me. I was isolated and victimized by the Victim's Response Unit. I learned how much world peace matters to the Peace Corps, not at all. I used to believe in the Peace Corps, and everything they stood for, but I see now I was alone in that. I genuinely believed in helping people, and here I was being punished by the Peace Corps for being a victim. The Peace Corps is purely a Propaganda Corp lead by trash that threatens victims, and military intelligence who recruit for the CIA. That is how the United States Peace Corps psychologically abused me. The Peace Corps ruined my life. And I almost died for them, but I still lost everything. I am calling them out on all their behind closed doors threats and everything they did to me. Pay attention and observe, everything I have written here is true, and I know they will deny it. You as a volunteer, pay attention and observe and plan. If you know their modus operandi, then you can plan and prepare.

There is an unofficial policy in the Peace Corps that must be exposed. If the Country Director abroad and the Victim's Response Unit in DC both use threats behind closed doors, then that means it is policy of the United States Peace Corps to lie to the public about the reality of the Peace Corps. I am telling the world, and here I am sacrificing myself once again for world peace. It was only after I was being sent back to America did the Country Director bother to report to DC. Only after, did they even consider moving me to another site. Only after, did a psychologist call me. Not when I reported everything, but after I was being medically evacuated. The Country Director's actions are approved of by the Peace Corps and the US government and the US congress. Why did the Country Director do all this to silence me? Why all the manipulation and behind closed door tactics? The Peace Corps is above the law and does not care. I almost died for them, and they abused, manipulated, intimidated, and threatened me. This is policy and procedure, they silence victims and reports in country, and if that does not work, they will silence victims in DC by threat. They keep all reports contained to protect their image. The Peace Corps serves its image first, as propaganda should.

Throughout the med-evac process, the Peace Corps in DC is in communication with the Peace Corps in country, and they all have to decide if they want the volunteer back. The Country Director shortened my return permission from 45 days to 42 days stating that I needed to attend a conference, and if I couldn't attend, he would not want me back in the program. It was an excuse; they always find an excuse. He put an additional provision on me, saying that if I came back, I would have to sign a contract saying I would study Georgian every month with a language teacher. I was already taking lessons with a Georgian teacher and had passed all language exams. Why was he forcing me to sign a contract forcing me to study Georgian when I already was? As policy, the Peace Corps forces volunteers to sign language training contracts as a tool to terminate volunteers. It is a victim blaming measure as many times the Peace Corps blames victims by saying whatever happened, was caused by the volunteer's language skills. No one forces you to sign a contract for your well-being. By forcing volunteers to sign, they have another bureaucratic reason to terminate volunteers, and documentation that the volunteer has language problems. You are forced under pressure to sign a contract or face termination. By forcing you to sign, they show that you agree with them, that you need to improve your language, and they will blame you for your language skills. This came from the Country Director who openly refused to study the language of the country he was the director of. It is a purely punitive move for a bureaucracy, but they say it is for the safety of the volunteer. This is apparent in the fact I was almost drowned to death by another, and the Country Director used this measure against me, as if I could speak when drowning, and when I was already taking lessons. The Peace Corps uses these contracts against volunteers and whatever happened was the volunteer's fault because of the language. The Peace Corps blames the victim any chance they get. Why would they have me sign a contract when I was already studying, and after I almost died for them? This was irrelevant, because I had passed all my language exams to the satisfaction of the Peace Corps, with no problems and actively sought out tutoring and language classes any chance I could get. They did this to protect themselves. I did not sign because they medically discharged me anyway. The other option is termination if you choose to not sign, and they will blame you for that as well. If you want to learn how to blame the victim, join the Peace Corps.

After you are medically terminated out of the Peace Corps, they have to make a decision on your benefits. If you survive longer than a year as a volunteer, the Peace Corps has to find a legal reason to deny your benefits. Before one year, they do not need a reason and will terminate the volunteer without cause, no benefits received. I was past the one-year mark. The Country Director tried to cancel my benefits, but he could not. Before he spoke with us at the final phone call before I was discharged, he called my school that I served at, to clarify I was doing my work. I was. For the past year, I had been marching through snowstorms at night to lesson plan, showing up on time every day, managing several projects and clubs, and helping other volunteers on their projects. Even on top of all the medical problems I faced, I still did the best I could. The principal told the Country Director I was doing my job. The Country Director then called the next town over to check and see what the super intendent thought of me. He called a site that was not even mine to a director that was not mine, to dig up any dirt he could. The super intendent said that I was a good volunteer and always came to help out. They will look for any excuse they can. They could find nothing on me.

The Country Director said the following over the phone at the Victim Response Unit's office, "You did it, you made it past the year mark, just barely, so I am granting you the Returned Peace Corps Volunteers status." This is the RPCV status, kind of like an honorable discharge. This means you have lifelong benefits in the Peace Corps, if you want to go back. The US Government and the Peace Corps declared my mission a success and I completed my service to America. If you do not get that, it looks bad on your record, especially if they have to find a reason. Many of his own staff signed recommendation letters for me, Program Managers, Trainers, even people from NGO's I worked with gave me recommendation letters, and other volunteers. I did my job for the Peace Corps, the doctor saw me psychologically fit for duty, and they gave me my benefits after medically discharging me, and after threatening to prosecute me.

I filled in the Description of Service for my benefits, to be signed off by the Country Director, it needed his signature, and everything else was filled out. He signed it two weeks after I turned it in. He sat on it for two weeks, which is a bureaucrat's way of saying "fuck you." A long time for a signature, but short enough to not draw questions. He reduced my 52 weeks of benefits for government jobs; he reduced it by two weeks with this tactic, and it shows you how petty he really is, even after abusing a victim. They declared my mission a success and could not find fault. The government declared me a success in the Peace Corps. The Peace Corps is a joke. They tried to silence me, and they all failed.

ALWAYS LOOK LIKE YOU ARE HELPING

The last contact I had with the Country Director was through email, after I had all my documents signed. I was collecting recommendation letters, and I had everyone who I worked with, trainers, managers, directors of NGOs, and other volunteers. I am not an idiot when it comes to the Country Director, I knew him better than any volunteer. I knew he would not give me a recommendation letter, but I still asked him for one. Why would I ask a man who psychologically abused me after I almost died for the Peace Corps? To see what he would say. He did not disappoint. He replied by not saying "no" directly. Instead, he suggested that I ask managers who I worked closer with and who knew me better. That is when I learned the truth about the Peace Corps: always appear to be helping to avoid responsibility. Before I became a volunteer, he terminated a volunteer from the year before, then he helped that ex-volunteer find work in Georgia. All to look like he was helping, when in reality he was harming. How else do you explain being manipulated and abused, and then threatened with prosecution after I almost died serving America. That is the mindset and the purpose of the Peace Corps. They help to avoid responsibility.

The purpose of the Peace Corps is to make America look like it is helping; that is the image. This is why the doctors do not diagnose. This is why the Peace Corps has psychologists, to appear to help for 45 days, and then dump the injured volunteer off on their own. It is all to appear to help, without actually helping. It is cheap and avoids responsibility. There is no after-service care for volunteers, because the Peace Corps does not care.

POST-SERVICE

NULL

The Peace Corps has known about the post-service problems for years, and has done nothing. There is no excuse for how the US government and the Peace Corps treats Returned Peace Corps Volunteers when they need medical care. This is all the proof you need to know how little they care about their volunteers. If they cared, they would not have volunteers go through the nightmare that I and so many others had to. There is no healthcare after Peace Corps. Once you are out, you are done and on your own, they do not care about you. You can choose to **buy** a terrible healthcare package that lasts a month. That is your reward as a volunteer, you can buy terrible health insurance for a month. I have been told how useless the insurance is by many volunteers, I did not bother. That is the American way, you serve them for free, and they turn around to sell you something. There is nothing cheaper than the Peace Corps.

For volunteers who need medical help from their service, the Peace Corps tells them to enroll in workers compensation through the federal website and fill out the information. The Peace Corps no longer does anything and the volunteer is now dealing with the Department of Labor, which does not care about you or your service, even if you almost died for America. The Peace Corps tells you to go to a website and that is it. If I thought Peace Corps bureaucrats were bad, these people are the worst, and you are forced to deal with them to take care of your medical problems. The Peace Corps says you are medically covered for your service, do not believe them, this is where they are proven liars. For the medical problems I was discharged for by the Peace Corps and the US government, I was denied treatment for by the government and the Department of Labor. All the injuries I had sustained, they denied. The medical problems they kicked me out for, they denied treatment for. This is what my sacrifice meant. This was with a diagnosis from different Ohio doctors and these bureaucrats overruled the doctors, saying it was not from my service, despite documentation. These entrance level pencil jockeys overruled medical doctors. A medical professional with a medical degree was overruled by a government employee who might not even have a bachelor's degree; this is what to expect from being injured while serving America in the Peace Corps. This is how they treat Returned Peace Corps Volunteers. There is no appeal, they deny and prevent you from getting the treatment you need for the problems you received from serving in the Peace Corps, from serving America. Denial is your reward for your sacrifice and risking your life.

All those problems I mentioned that went unresolved, they got worse. All my injuries occurred while I served and was promised by the Peace Corps that they would be taken care of, the Peace Corps lied, and they knew what would happen when they told me. The Peace Corps lies. They accepted the case but denied treatment. They repeatedly denied my injury claims and said it was because of something else, like my weight and not my injuries, despite medical documentation, several diagnoses, and doctors pointing to the obvious answers. I had gained weight after coming back to America due to a selection of food beyond the potato mixed with severe depression, anxiety, and my trauma from the Peace Corps Country Director developed further. The Stress Disorder I had got worse. Doctors ordered physical therapy, medical procedures, and operations while non-medically trained bureaucrats overruled them and diagnosed everything as a weight problem. A bureaucrat made a medical diagnosis on an injury I had lived with and needed treatment for over a year, just said no, and that was it. When pressed on how a back injury could be affected by weight, he denied the treatment without reason.

I served my country and was injured, and they said I had to pay for it myself. I had to pay for my own physical therapy for my back and pay for numerous medical procedures and operations by myself. Luckily, I had a good therapist who treated it right the first week, he understood it was nerve damage.

I got a job at a bank immediately after the Peace Corps as I had bank experience. The doctors pointed out what was wrong immediately and the treatment I paid for helped, not because of the Peace Corps, but because I had to do it myself. I still have the back problem, a permanent reminder of my service to the Peace Corps. I had to pay for my own treatment from injuries that I received while serving the Peace Corps. The injuries were well documented, but a bureaucrat without any medical training can overrule a doctor, and this claims examiner stated that he did not see how an injury from a year ago could still affect me. The doctors explained everything, and they still said no. This is America. It is pointless to serve America. I spent over $6,000.00 the year after my Peace Corps service on medical bills alone, with insurance I paid for, from injuries I sustained from the Peace Corps. To put it in perspective, from ages 18 to 26, the age I joined the Peace Corps, I had spent less than $1,000.00 for the eight years before I joined the Peace Corps. I was in perfect health before, and after, my body was wrecked. For all they denied, I spent more than my entire readjustment allowance on my medical problems alone, and spent my own savings trying to fix what the Peace Corps and the US government caused me. Thank you, Peace Corps, for wasting my time and money, and telling me my service was worthless. The Peace Corps cheated me out of thousands of dollars, they are thieves.

As for my digestive track, I went to one doctor who pointed the problem out immediately. It was an obvious diagnosis. It would take a year before I received the surgery and only after months of tests to prove I still had a medical necessity and the government dragging their feet. It took two years to get the surgery I needed from when the problem started in service. The Peace Corps has a proud history of medical failure and they should be ashamed of their duplicity. Worse, the medical bills were still being sent to me as I started writing this, as the Department of Labor refused to pay for the operation after they approved and took two more years to resolve that issue. Serving in the Peace Corps ruined my life.

I sacrificed more for my service to the Peace Corps, than people who spent three years in the Peace Corps. I lost so much serving America that I regret my service in the Peace Corps, it is not worth it. This is how I lived my life thanks to the Peace Corps. I would have to deal with these problems for over two years after my service, longer than my service, with all the medical paperwork because the Department of Labor is too lazy to make a call themselves to fix a numerical error in the paperwork. Somewhere, someone messed up the paperwork on medical coding, and if you know anything about that, it is extremely common to the point you can get a degree in medical coding, it is that complex, and the errors are common. I had to spend hundreds of hours on the phone arguing to get the medical treatment I needed, that is not hyperbole. I spent every lunch hour every day arguing over the phone. I was constantly denied, told to wait, told it is my problem not theirs, they blamed everything they could on me, after everything. I had to work through the American medical system learning how the system worked to get it done myself. This made my transition back to America far worse. I became embittered more than any other point in my life. I had lived for two years with stomach pain before the issue was resolved, two years, because I chose to serve my country.

Every day, I would have to wait ten minutes on the phone tree alone, to leave a message to wait for a call back from the bureaucrat, daily, as I had to get the right numbers in the right places and report back to the medical coding person at the hospital. I had to be the middle man for their failures as they refused to talk to anyone but me, and it was not always like this, they cheapened the system. The Department of Labor would not call anyone, not doctors, not the hospitals, nothing. The hospitals were perfectly happy to call, but the Department of Labor refuses to speak with them directly, it is only to avoid paying medical bills that they do this. They do not receive emails from the outside, they only have to call you, the claimant, back once after you call, and you have to wait for them when they call or else you have to start the whole process over.

This system is designed to prevent payment for medical services. They treat Returned Peace Corps Volunteers who served their country like garbage. They could not pick up the phone to call the hospital or anyone else, it was all up to me and me alone, because they did not have to. I had to talk with every single billing official from the hospital, and back and forth with the Department of Labor for years. Every single lunchbreak every day I would be doing this. I was dropped off alone by the Peace Corps to deal with this system. They do not warn you. I left the Peace Corps, and it suddenly became as if they did not know who I was or the fact I almost died for them.

The Department of Labor was partially privatized, so a politically connected person made a ton of money off of making my life miserable. That is what serving America means. It would be years before everything was resolved, it would be years after I left the Peace Corps, and how much I endured for them, over three years of medical bills, hundreds of hours on the phone. The Department of Labor had to change the phone tree because I figured out the short cuts and started calling the managers and leaving messages for them, forcing them to be legally responsible. I kept coming back every single day to get this situation resolved, because they were not doing their job. This is what the Peace Corps did to me. This is your reward for almost losing your life for them. Years of anxiety, fear, work just to get the medical care I needed. The Peace Corps has a nice smiling face, they only care about that smile and not doing the bare minimum to help their own people. I am still anxious there is a bill somewhere dragging down my credit score. Imagine waking up one day to getting a bill for $20,000, and the government said the surgery was approved, but they denied it after the surgery already happened. That was my life. They refused it again and again and again, and they do not want to pay for anything. If America treats its own people like this, then America is doomed to fall.

From my Peace Corps service, I would have to undergo multiple surgeries, multiple procedures, dozens of doctors' visits, pay for my own therapy, two whole surgeries on my own, and several procedures, and all thanks to the Peace Corps. I spent more time dealing with all the billing problems and denials than the actual timed I served. By the end of it all, I had become embittered at believing in America and the Peace Corps. I regret serving America, I regret serving in the United States Peace Corps, and this is because of how lazy and irresponsible they are. The Peace Corps, its rich kid propaganda backed by military intelligence who threatens victims. I can say that fairly after everything they did to me, after everything I went through, for them, and in good faith on my part. The Peace Corps is a Machiavellian machine. They say grass roots movement, it is colonial astroturfing.

I would love to approach the section with a calm demeanor based on peace, as is my nature. However, when I come to this section, I am reminded of how much I had to go through just to get a surgery I needed while I served, how many years of my life wasted on a callous system. This system is an abject failure of the US government, and the Peace Corps, and all parties involved should be publicly disgraced. My life was ruined by the Peace Corps, and after everything I went through, and even after I almost lost my life. There is no other way to express the anger. It is fair.

I regret my service, I regret serving America, I regret joining the Peace Corps off of this alone, let alone everything else that happened. I do not regret helping people. I believed in volunteer work and had over three hundred hours of volunteer service before I even joined the Peace Corps. No one deserves this treatment. I will turn people away when they speak of wanting to serve in the Peace Corps. I tell them my story. I tell them stories of women being raped and sexually assaulted. I tell them the story of a young woman doing her best to serve her country and help kids get out of a sexually exploited situation, only to get murdered because a Peace Corps employee called the sexual predator who went and killed her. I tell them the story of Deborah Gardener who was murdered for refusing to have sex. The Peace Corps is proof no-good deed goes unpunished.

TRANSITION BACK TO AMERICA

My life had fallen into blackness. I could no longer see any life I could lead. I could not connect to any person around me, relate to anyone, or to any group or even my own country. Wherever I went, I felt alienated. I could not form relationships with anyone anymore. I went from useless job to useless job, no longer believing in anything.

Before the Peace Corps, I didn't miss a Sunday of church in twenty years. After Peace Corps, I did not even believe in God. Where once I spent at least five hours every week doing volunteer work, now nothing. I became a nihilist, nothing mattered. With my experience from the Peace Corps, my anxiety and fear of being attacked by supervisors and colleagues mounted daily. I had flashbacks, I had flashbacks when dealing with supervisors. I grew anxious around coworkers. I grew anxious realizing I could be harmed at any moment as no one followed rules or laws, and I would be blamed for anything and everything. I became a victim, believing I was powerless and anyone could do anything to me, after all, the Peace Corps did everything they wanted without consequence.

Where once I was constantly doing my best in everything I did, down to the smallest detail and following every rule possible, now, I did not even show up to work on time. Before, I arrived five minutes early for everything, now I was late by twenty minutes. What did it matter how hard I worked? I would be attacked anyway, and blamed for it, and everything taken away. Where before I graduated top of my university with honors while working, now I did not care about any career or anything, it would be taken from me. I could not build relationships with anyone around me, they would abuse me, or alienate me and tell me to shut up. Other volunteers who I thought I could trust, silenced me when I spoke about what happened. I could not trust anyone.

It grew to the point that I broke down crying, having a flashback after being yelled at by a supervisor while on the job. I could no longer function in America. I do not believe in America, not after everything. I now had no future. I broke down by the week with flashbacks. Even at my closest friend's apartment, I could be found curled into a ball crying. I was having flashbacks. I do not remember these periods during, I just remembering being shaken by a friend and told what happened. I laugh because they told me I could reapply to the Peace Corps, I had spent so long dealing with my medical problems because the department of labor kept denying everything over and over, the application timeline expired, but they knew that would happen. They would not accept me anyway. Any mental record is a permanent ban. So, the Peace Corps gave me false hope, and that is what their image is, false hope propaganda.

I could not go back to my home, as the Peace Corps so ingrained it into me during indoctrination, I was homeless. I came back to where I was born, but I felt like a stranger in my own homeland. It is far better to be a stranger in a strange land, than a stranger in your homeland. I could not relate to anyone anymore. I could not feel anything, no emotional attachment anymore. I felt nothing, no love, no growth, no anything. Everyone I loved and cared for was on the other side of the planet, and they had been taken from me. Where once I believed in the Peace Corps, they had isolated and abused me behind closed doors. Where once I loved my country like my grandfather, thanked every veteran I met, I did not care about America at all. My friends in the Peace Corps, those I could relate to, were now gone, and I came back to Ohio. I could not relate to anyone. I was in pain, and dealing with all the stress of the Department of Labor, and all the problems from the Peace Corps. I felt absolutely alone. I had no future, I had no one I could relate to. The Peace Corps isolated me. My country did not care, and I almost lost my life for them. That is what I learned from the Peace Corps, no one cared.

I could not sleep most nights, and I could not feel anything at all. I could maybe sleep four hours a night if I was lucky, and I woke from nightmares constantly. The world went black. I found myself drinking heavily to try and sleep. I drank to black out because I did not want to be conscious anymore and I was tired of dealing with it all. I drank so much I could not breathe; I was drowning myself in alcohol. All my friends were gone, my "home" from the Peace Corps was gone. I was emotionally involved in that place and the people, and through it all I did my best to help them. Now I had no connection to any of that world anymore. I was treated like leper by the Peace Corps, while dealing with all my medical problems.

I hated my life and everything I had lived through. I wished I had died in that river. Blamed for it all, I had no future left. I had survived almost being murdered in the Peace Corps, harassed to the point of assault by a volunteer, psychologically abused by a Peace Corps Country Director and threatened with criminal prosecution by the Peace Corps Victim's Unit, then abandoned when I was in need of surgery. I joined the Peace Corps and got interrogated by military intelligence, a CIA plant. Then kicked out unceremoniously and left to deal with the world's worst healthcare system brought to you by the Peace Corps. My life was over, I was helpless to do anything. I tried drinking myself to death multiple times and it did not work.

I came back a different person. I felt like I was locked inside of my head watching myself drown all over again. I started overeating, and I had put on fifty pounds of weight, while still having stomach problems. I started womanizing. Where once I would not even have sex without a long-term relationship, now, I picked up women in bars. Dating apps, bars, college women, all of it was the same to me. Female friends I had had for years, I used for sex and hated myself each time. I used my own friends for sex. Friends I had for over ten years I drove away from me. I hurt my best friends. I wished I had died in that river. I ended up destroying friendships I had for years. People I loved I used for sex, I hated myself so much. This was not me. I destroyed my oldest friendship. All dignity was stripped from me in the Peace Corps, and I came back that way. To my friends who I hurt, if they read this, please understand what I went through, and who came back.

I could not feel anything. This is where the Peace Corps brought me. When they paid me my returned stipend, they told me they over paid by a few hundred dollars, and asked for me to return it. They took money from my bank account without my permission and asked for permission only after. I did everything they asked and they still ruined my life. They buried me and tried to cover me up with threats and intimidation. The Peace Corps threatens victims, because their image is more important than the truth. They did this to me. Victim blaming is policy in the Peace Corps, expect no different.

THE CLICK

I saw no future and no point in living anymore. After you leave the Peace Corps, they give you a return allowance of several thousand dollars depending on how long you served. I walked into a sporting goods store. I told the clerk I wanted a shotgun. He showed me a nice collection of guns. I had to admit I wanted to buy the double-barrel side-by-side as I liked the old west motif. Instead, I went with the cheapest twelve gauge I could find. I knew it would be destroyed afterwards anyway, so buying something nice was wasting money. I grabbed some buckshot, shook the clerks' hands, thanked him for being nice to me, and walked to my car. I do not think they ever expected someone to walk in and buy a gun for the purposes I had in mind. I went to the store and bought vodka. I went into a restaurant, and had a nice cheeseburger and milkshake.

I drove out of town to some old woods. I left a note beforehand on my desk in a room I was renting, it said where I could be found. I did not want to ruin the property value of the house; the landlord was nice to me. That is what my return home was, denial of medical help while living in pain, unable to feel, afraid of the world around me. That is what my life became, a living hell thanks to the Peace Corps. I do not know how many Peace Corps Volunteers kill themselves after service. I do know the Peace Corps does not want to know or talk about it. I parked my car and walked with my hiking backpack, loaded with vodka, a shotgun and shells, out into the woods. No one was around. It was a semi-cool day, I was wearing my jacket, it was cloudy. I walked off the path behind a hill, and walked into a small clearing and sat down against a tree. No one would find me by accident.

Killing yourself is an inhuman effort. You have to force yourself to not think about what was going to happen, you have to force yourself to do it. I comforted myself, "it's ok, I'll be at peace soon." Do not worry, just do it, just move on. I lifted the barrel, put it in my mouth. Just trying to 'move on' as the Peace Corps Country Director told me to. *How will this help?* An intrusive thought kept hitting me. *How will this help those who will suffer like you?* It was the voice in my head, I did not know whose. I fell into a different blackness. I broke down crying, arguing with myself. *Will this help anyone?* By this point I had not slept for two days. I had not slept well since I came back. *How will this help people like you?* I collapsed, shaking and crying.

I came to sometime later. I do not know if I blacked out, or if I had a flashback, or both. I was woozy and the sky was darker. No one was around. I looked around and remembered what I was doing. *How will this help those who will suffer like you?* This was the part of me that had survived intact, the part that refuses to die, and comes out fighting. *How will this help those who will suffer like you? All those who believe in you and who have built you up, will their efforts go in vain?* I relented to it; I could not let my loved one's efforts waste into oblivion. Killing myself would not fix anything, it would end everything, but this would waste all the effort everyone put into me, and only harm the people I loved. It would only help the people who have harmed me. Killing myself would have only helped the US government and the Peace Corps, that is where my life had led me. My own country did not care. I walked back to my car. I would not permit myself to drive drunk, or even exhausted for fear of taking another's life. Even at my bleakest I still had a code.

THE TWITCHING EYE

If you do not kill yourself, you have to climb out of hell a handful of dirt at a time. I worked full time, to pay off my student debt, taking care of the Peace Corps' injuries, having flashbacks, and undergoing multiple surgeries, sometimes two a month. I was someone else. I was someone else for as long as that eye twitched, ever since the interrogation. Volunteers will go through hell to serve, only for their good faith and deeds to be used as propaganda. I served in good faith, but that does not matter to the Peace Corps.

What did it feel like? I was still drowning. You are locked away in your own head while some other consciousness controls you. You watch your life like it is a horror show where you are the main star. It is horrifying. You do not have control. You can shout in your head all you want, but the thing in control is deaf. The Peace Corps turned me into someone I hated. It would be years before I found help and a way out. I became someone I did not want to be. I became a womanizing alcoholic, or an alcoholic womanizer, with a twitching eye.

I had no community and lived through hell, and now it had taken its toll on me. All the trauma caused by everything, suddenly losing my community, after working so hard to serve. My mind was broken. I should have died in that river. That is what I thought, I should have died serving America, and that is where my life took me. By trying to be good,

I ended up losing everything. No good deed... what the Peace Corps did to me, destroyed everything. I will never serve America again.

I have been paralyzed, unable to function because of what they did to me. These problems I received while serving out of my own sense of patriotic duty. The Peace Corps is not worth it. America is not worth it. I am still here, reliving these events over and over and over. Unable to grow and move forward. That is where the Peace Corps left me, a broken and silent man watching the years go by, a silent victim of the Peace Corps. No longer able to feel or live in the present. I loved America so much, then they did this to me. That is what the Peace Corps did for me. A drunken suicidal womanizer, that is what my service to America, and what the Peace Corps made me into.

THE PEACE CORPS SERVES THEIR IMAGE FIRST

Never believe that someone is a good person because they were in the Peace Corps. I do not thank Peace Corps Volunteers. Once, a marine thanked me, I thanked him for his sentiment, but reassured him his sacrifice was greater than mine could have ever been. On many occasions I have met Returned Peace Corps Volunteers who have flat out refused to even hear my story and told others not to listen to me. My own trauma and my fellow Returned Peace Corps Volunteers told me to shut up, denying what I lived through. All the abuse I survived, and how much of my life was destroyed because of the Peace Corps and I was told to shut up.

It is always white volunteers who served in Africa, the center of the Peace Corps image. I have been told by Returned Peace Corps Volunteers, "You shouldn't tell that story", "Don't listen to him (referring to me in front of me)," or "what's wrong with you", "the Peace Corps isn't like that", "But think of all the good you did." Some just told me to "shut up." I almost lost my life, and the Peace Corps ruined the rest of it, and other volunteers were telling me to shut up. They are a testament to the Peace Corps image. All of this after I tell how horrible my life had become.

I could not relate to other returned volunteers. The ones who publicly silence me are always white people who served in Africa who express their immense emotional joy of helping poor black children, the image of the Peace Corps. They talk about their love of helping people, then turn and silence me. I have to ask the question, is the pinnacle of being a good white person in America tied up to helping poor black people in Africa? Then there is a racial element to the image. If that is the case, then their ego is tied up with that racial image, that propaganda, and my life is a threat to their ego. I am not talking about all volunteers, only the ones who tried to silence me, and that false image the Peace Corps presents itself as. Why else would they silence me? They are Peace Corps fanatics living in denial about the reality. To deny what I had to live through, only points to some cognitive dissonance. These people are nothing more than White Saviors, and the image of the Peace Corps is a white savior bureaucracy. That is what that image is and the image needs to end. Why is it always poor black children? Why not just poor children? There is a racial element there. Look closely at that image you will start to see things about it. Is the Peace Corps image an extension of White Man's Burden? I don't know if these people suffer from white guilt, or live in denial about how America came to exist by colonization, slavery, genocide, and ethnic cleansing. Minorities in America are second class citizens, why don't we teach that abroad? There is something about that Peace Corps image that is unsettling, once you know the reality behind the closed doors. Look closely at it.

There is a hypocritical elitist element to that image as well. In America, we strip any assistance from the poor, and blame them for being lazy or stupid. Meanwhile, Americans economically colonize foreign countries and keep them poor, and then Americans praise themselves for volunteering in the Peace Corps. Why do we not blame them for being poor? Instead, we say they need help, when we let the poor die in the streets in America. These are questions about that image that need to be asked. There is a double standard in the Peace Corps' America.

The Peace Corps has always been political propaganda. JFK started it to get votes from college kids. When it was started, its design was to spread American idealism when the Soviet Union was at its peak and more countries were turning towards the communism. It was counter propaganda, created to combat the Domino Effect. It has always been politically motivated propaganda and to train future diplomats. That is the purpose. JFK was not an altruist; he was a philanderer who supported the Civil Rights Movement to counter communist propaganda. Now, it is to keep foreigners believing in America, via American Exceptionalism. The more they believe in US, the higher the value of our dollar. It all comes back to money, the heart of the capitalist culture.

Peace Corps feminism it the key to understanding that the Peace Corps is propaganda. Deborah Gardner was a Peace Corps Volunteer who was murdered within twenty years of the Peace Corps' founding, by a male volunteer who killed her because she refused to have sex with him. She was stabbed 22 times. The Peace Corps aided and abetted a woman murderer to protect their own image, then they preach feminism and equality abroad. The Peace Corps even said the murderer's mission was a success and gave him a Completion of Service form. This is hypocrisy on a grand scale. Women are still paid 7/10 of a man in America, and the federal government just took away a woman's right to her own body. Then the federal government then goes out and preaches gender equality and promotes feminism in the Peace Corps. It is hypocrisy and propaganda. They helped a murderer get away with his crime. The Peace Corps is as morally bankrupt as the rest of the US government.

Peace Corps Georgia is a continuation of the cold war propaganda machine. The only reason it is in Georgia is to destabilize Russian influence and spread American influence. That was why they put a CIA spy as a Country Director. Why else would he recruit for the CIA while in the Peace Corps? Another country director in South America asked volunteers to collect information on foreigners. All volunteers play "guess the spy" against other volunteers. The spies are the country directors, but not every country has a spy or needs one. Even on a bureaucratic level it was obvious. According to the CIA, Georgia is a middle-eastern country, not European. The Country Director spoke Farsi and worked in military intelligence in Afghanistan right before coming to Peace Corps Georgia, then he tried to recruit an Arabic speaking volunteer for the CIA. If you go back and check the recorded phone calls with JFK, he refers specifically to the volunteer group when keeping spies out, not the government employees. The Peace Corps is nothing more than propaganda and a recruiting ground. The volunteers do not serve world peace, they serve only to sway public opinion towards America. Soft diplomacy is the name if you like technical terms.

The Peace Corps is used in eastern Europe to break apart Russian influence and spread NATO's military goals, and that is the only reason it is in Eastern Europe, as Peace Corps Eastern Europe started with the fall of the USSR, and NATO spread to every country the Peace Corps went into, to prepare them to transition from the Soviet system. There was a Peace Corps Russia for a short time, but that was never designed to be part of NATO, that was to spread American influence into the Russian population. Eastern European countries are too far developed to reason anything else.

Meanwhile, the American government keeps foreign countries in poverty by taking their resources and kills off their leaders who try and change it. All while the Peace Corps Volunteers show how great America is by helping them. The very definition of duplicity, it is a Machiavellian Machine. Keep them in poverty and then help them a little bit, enough to avoid responsibility. The Peace Corps says it is designed to fight colonization, the colonization of other countries, only to replace it with the economic colonization of America. The Peace Corps is the helping hand that holds poor countries down. American culture hates the poor of America and yet we glorify helping the poor of other countries. Why?

The human race is developing and globalizing, and as the world moves forward, the Peace Corps will become irrelevant as America falls further from power. These Peace Corps white saviors are the worst, they talk about how great they are and the Peace Corps, yet they try to silence any dissent. The Peace Corps has reports of crimes from all over, yet they refuse to act on them, or blame the victim, and they suppress any reports that come out. Peace Corps employees have blamed women for rape. Peace Corps, making people believe America is exceptional, even at the cost of helping murderers and threatening victims. The Peace Corps is a white savior bureaucracy with grass roots propaganda and colonial astroturfing. There is no glory in dying for America, it is a waste of a life.

Dying for the Peace Corps is useless, you get your name in a lobby. For all the harm I was done by the Peace Corps, and how much trauma, lost time, and financial ruin they caused me, I would never volunteer for the Peace Corps again, even if they paid me.

I have often wondered why some Returned Peace Corps Volunteers are so keen on silencing me, and telling me not to tell my story. Some have encouraged me to speak out, others have tried to silence me. I finally figured it out, it's cognitive dissonance. Fanatics do not come from the military, they come from the Peace Corps, as the Peace Corps fosters a fanatic culture. Peace Corps Volunteers are told they serve the greatest country on earth, yet they have to deal with the realization that America routinely commits war crimes and supports genocide. Yet the Peace Corps Volunteers have to deal with the cognitive dissonance of serving in the Peace Corps, serving the same government that does what the Peace Corps says they are against. They are told, "be yourself but don't", even before they are volunteers. In order to deal with this cognitive dissonance, they sweep dissent under the rug, and say the Peace Corps is flawless and America is the greatest country on Earth. In doing so, they silence victims.

Volunteers have to deal with all the positive memories of helping people, and then deal with the fact that they have been used in deceiving foreigners into believing that America is a kind and loving country that cares about them, when in reality, all they have served as is propaganda. They view themselves as the pinnacle of morality on earth for serving in the Peace Corps, attaching their egos to a bureaucratic machine, and any harm to the Peace Corps is a harm to them. Burying reports and silencing victims is as much of the Peace Corps as is learning a foreign language. These are American fanatics. Conquering the hearts and minds for American corporations. That is what the Peace Corps boils down to, conquering. The Peace Corps is colonization, the subtle American way. Convincing poor foreigners that America is looking out for them, when chances are the CIA stole any future that culture could have had in some move to obtain cheap resources, or stop democratic movements or the nationalization of said resources. Then the Peace Corps comes to save the day. No wonder they choose the easy option of trying to silence me.

The reality is so much worse to deal with. It all starts with "be yourself, but don't." They believe in that so much. If you look at the Peace Corps jobs website, you can even find postings for positions at Guantanamo. Be yourself, but don't.

Why did I write all of this out? Why did I relive all of this over and over again for years, the most painful memories of my life, to risk my life by writing this, ending my life in America permanently, throwing away any hope of a life in my own homeland? So other volunteers know what to expect, so they know what can happen to them and they can plan and prepare. Pay attention, because I have written out everything here. Watch how the Peace Corps reacts and responds to this. I am dragging them out into the open, and I want you to see what they do, so you can know how they operate. They will deny and discredit me anyway they can, and I am sure they will get as many fanatic volunteers and others to deny what happened to me. Watch how they operate. This is the US government, and they do not tolerate whistleblowers.

I am calling them out on their threat. The Peace Corps threatened me with criminal prosecution after I was abused by them, and after I almost died for them. I want to see them deny that threat in which case they will never be able to threaten anyone again. Or, I want to them to carry out their threat so we can bring everything into the open. I have nothing left to lose. I do not want volunteers walking in believing the propaganda. The Peace Corps is a Machiavellian Machine. I believed in them once, and they took everything. They abused me, lied to me, and ruined my life, after my health deteriorated, and after I almost lost my life for them by the people I came to help, and manipulated by the program I loved and believed in. They silenced me, took away my voice, and left me a broken man. They invited me in and abused me. For how much the Peace Corps does for victims, that black granite memorial might as well say, "They volunteered for it." I know, because I was seconds away from having my name immortalized in a lobby. That is why.

Patrick Shea RPCV

Printed in the USA
CPSIA information can be obtained
at www.ICGtesting.com
LVHW090838090724
784993LV00001B/53